WHO ★ WOULD ★ WIN?

WHO
★ WOULD ★
WIN?

A GUIDE TO GREAT
IMAGINARY
SHOWDOWNS

PRESENTED BY
★ JUSTIN HEIMBERG ★

METRO BOOKS
NEW YORK

A QUIRK PACKAGING BOOK

© 2009 by Quirk Packaging, Inc.

This 2009 edition published by Metro Books,
by arrangement with Quirk Packaging, Inc.

Design by Lynne Yeamans
Editing by Lindsay Herman and Greg Chaput

Metro Books
122 Fifth Avenue
New York, NY 10011

ISBN: 978-1-4351-1058-8

Printed and bound in Singapore

10 9 8 7 6 5 4 3 2 1

★ CONTENTS ★

CHAPTER ONE
ARTS & LITERATURE
10

Michelangelo v Leonardo 12
The Question Mark v The Exclamation Point 14
Dr. Seuss v Shakespeare 16
Books v Movie Versions of Books 18
Pablo Picasso v Vincent Van Gogh 20
Red v Black 22
Ernest Hemingway v Norman Mailer 24
Verdana v Times New Roman 26
Yo Momma v Yo-Yo Ma 28
Quick Debates: Culture Clashes 30

CHAPTER TWO
SPORTS & LEISURE
32

1972 Miami Dolphins v 1985 Chicago Bears 34
Beer v Wine 36
Cookie Monster v Pac-Man 38
Muhammad Ali v Mike Tyson 40

Well-Done v Rare 42

Summer Games v Winter Games 44

Salt v Pepper 46

Quick Debates: Food Fights to the Finish 48

The Easter Bunny v Santa Claus 50

Björn Borg v Andre Agassi 52

Apples v Oranges 54

Hulk Hogan v The Rock 56

Meat Eaters v Vegetarians 58

The Boston Celtics v The LA Lakers 60

Quick Debates: Face-Offs Across Time 62

Hot Dog v Hamburger 64

Tea v Coffee 66

Crosswords v Sudoku 68

The Burger King v McDonaldland Characters 70

Rock v Paper v Scissors 72

CHAPTER THREE
HISTORY & POLITICS 74

Gandhi v Mother Teresa 76

Ross Perot v Ralph Nader 78

Jean-Paul Sartre v Socrates 80

Hammurabi v The U.S. Founding Fathers 82

Jimmy Carter v George W. Bush 84

Canada v Switzerland 86

Quick Debates: Military Match-Ups 88

Samurai v Ninja 90

George Washington v Abraham Lincoln 92

The '80s v The '90s 94

CHAPTER FOUR
ENTERTAINMENT
96

James Bond v Jason Bourne 98

Actors Turned Musicians v Musicians Turned Actors 100

Bruce Springsteen v Jon Bon Jovi 102

X-Men v Justice League 104

Clowns v Mimes 106

Cast of *Grease* v Cast of *High School Musical* 108

Dukes of Hazzard Uncle Jesse v *Full House* Uncle Jesse 110

Courtney Love v Amy Winehouse 112

King Kong v Godzilla 114

U2 v The Beatles 116

Quick Debates: Battle of the Bands 118

Smurfs v Care Bears 120

Dracula v Frankenstein's Monster 122

TomKat v Posh 'n' Becks v Bennifer 2.0 124

Captain Kirk v Captain Picard 126

Deadheads v Parrotheads 128

MacGyver v The A-Team 130
Quick Debates: Onscreen Fights to the Death 132
Fat Elvis v Skinny Elvis 134
Dumbledore v Gandalf 136
Guitarists v Drummers 138
The *300* Guys v The *Braveheart* Guys 140
The Terminator v Robocop 142
Art Garfunkel v John Oates 144
KITT v Optimus Prime 146

CHAPTER FIVE
SCIENCE & NATURE 148

Metric System v The American System of Measurement 150
Jupiter v Saturn 152
One Polar Bear v Fifty Koala Bears 154
Einstein v Newton 156
Crocodile v Lion 158
Quick Debates: The Survival of the Fittest 160
Left v Right 162
Balding v Taking Extreme Anti-Balding Measures 164
Summer v Winter 166
Brunch v Wind 168

Index 170

HOW TO USE THIS BOOK

In the following pages, you will find entertaining and insightful analyses of imaginary showdowns. Ever unbiased, the book offers argument for both sides, providing trivia, statistics, and factual background to help probe and explore the nooks and crannies of the duel in question. Combatants range from the invented to the historical, from immortal deities to household objects, all of which are forced to face off in hypothetical fights, battles, competitions, and comparisons.

Ultimately, *Who Would Win?* is a springboard for debate. The riffs, for and against, can jumpstart lively and vehement debate over trivial matters. We all need a rest from debating the big themes— religion, politics, current events, and other stuff that matters. It's time to focus our energies of persuasion on the inane and idiosyncratic.

While you can read the book alone, the debates it may spark are often best experienced with a group of friends, during which time allegiances, attitudes, and opinions will quickly emerge. Of course, much like more grandiose debates, these arguments can and will become personal and serious, and one is likely to find that a desk lamp has been thrown during an impassioned rant regarding the superiority of Captain Kirk over Captain Picard. Packed with sidebars that offer obscure-yet-fascinating facts (Didn't You Know?), Pop Quizzes, and even more fodder for debate (Quick Debates; Further Debate), *Who Would Win?* will guarantee hours and hours of fiery face-offs.

So, read, reason, react, and rebut. There are no holds barred here. Have at it.

CHAPTER ★ ONE ★

ARTS

&

LITERATURE

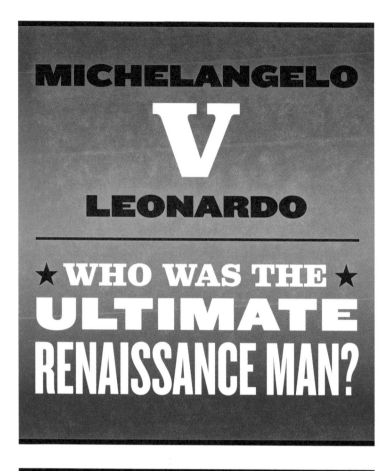

MICHELANGELO V LEONARDO

★ WHO WAS THE ★ ULTIMATE RENAISSANCE MAN?

THIS OR THAT:
Is It a Great Renaissance Artist or Pasta?

A. Botticelli   C. Bronzino   E. Gemelli

B. Casarecci   D. Gozzoli   F. Rigatoni

ANSWERS: a, c, and d. were Renaissance artists.

MICHELANGELO

By the time he was thirty, Michelangelo had finished what may be the two greatest works in the history of sculpture—the *Pieta* and the *David*—hits borne of young virtuosity unmatched until Michael Jackson's *Thriller* album debuted centuries later. These masterworks, though, are nothing compared with the **SISTINE CHAPEL**, far and away the world's most impressive frescoes in terms of quality and scope. Mind you, the Sistine Chapel was a diversion from Michelangelo's main task at the time, constructing the tomb of Pope Julius II, featuring the underrated statue of Moses (the biblical Moses, not Moses Malone). Finally, at the risk of turning this campaign negative, have you ever really looked at the *Mona Lisa*? Boring. Not even that hot.

LEONARDO

Leonardo da Vinci is the original **"RENAISSANCE MAN."** No mere painter, the man was also a mathematician, engineer, inventor, anatomist, portraitist, sculptor, architect, botanist, musician, writer, ladies' man, and man's man. And he did it all really well. That amount of success is the equivalent of Bill Gates also having a Top 40 hit, racking up NASCAR victories, and winning *Project Runway*. Leo defined his time while being way ahead of it. In his many notebooks (in which he wrote backward— how cool is that?!), he sketched prototypes of helicopters, solar-powered devices, plate tectonics, and calculators. Also included in his notebooks, we're told, are early renderings of the Big Mac and the prototype of the fair catch.

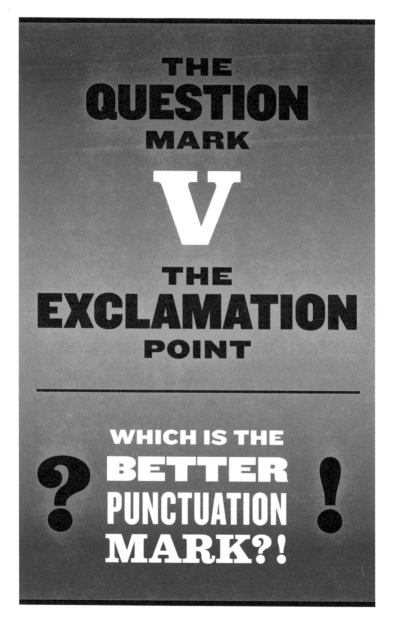

QUESTION MARK

What can you say about a symbol that always needs to yell to get its points across? What kind of vacuous content is exclamation point masking with its unwavering vehemence? Why can't it simply relax? What are the issues that drive this punctuation bully? What is it overcompensating for? Doesn't it have the least bit of **CURIOSITY**? Doesn't it have an iota of **WONDER** in the wide world? Does it merely shout to drown out the painful voices in its blood-rushed head? And have I not made my point? Or should I say "mark"?

EXCLAMATION POINT

Shut up! Stupid curvy wuss! *Oh, look at me and my inquisitive curious soul*! UP YOURS! Hey, we don't need your help, capitalization! I can just double up for extra **EMPHASIS**!! See, I **YELLED** that line!!! And that one even **LOUDER**! What's a question mark going to do, double up on itself for extra inquiry emphasis?? Look how dumb that looks! Point made! And watch your ass, comma! You're next!

FURTHER DEBATE

Italics v <u>Underline</u>?
The colon v The em dash?
& v 'n'?

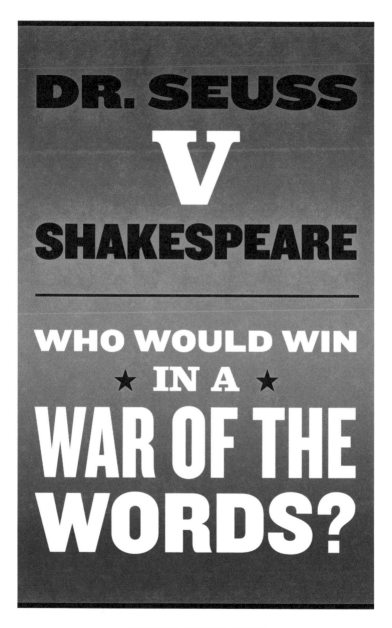

DR. SEUSS

V

SHAKESPEARE

WHO WOULD WIN
★ IN A ★
WAR OF THE
WORDS?

DR. SEUSS

Out damn spot, out I say!
I see spot run, I see spot stay
But try as I might, it won't wash away!
It's there in the night and there in the day!
Out damn spot, out I say!
Leave me, damned spot,
Go away!
Go away!
Go away!

SHAKESPEARE

I doth detest the emerald ovates and porcine dreck
I doth detest thou enclosed in rhomboid fury
I doth detest thou with vulpine guile coiled at my feet
I doth detest thou Sam of the Self Proclaimed

THIS OR THAT:
Is It a Dr. Seuss Character or a 1960s British Band?

A. The Lorax

B. The Whos of Whoville

C. The Troggs

D. Thidwick

E. Herman's Hermits

ANSWERS: c. and e. are bands.

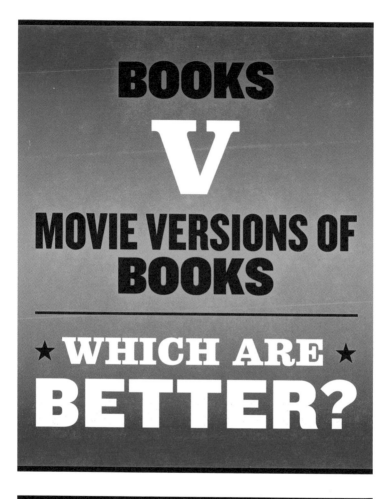

BOOKS

V

MOVIE VERSIONS OF BOOKS

★ WHICH ARE ★
BETTER?

FURTHER DEBATE: Better as a Book or a Movie?

The Godfather

Lord of the Rings

Booty Call

BOOKS

There is nothing like curling up in bed with a good book, enjoying the **LYRICAL LANGUAGE** of a master—a literary fest free of advertising and product placement. (What if *Moby Dick* contained the line, "'Call me Ishmael,' he said as he unwrapped a delicious Charleston Chew"?) Reading is a much more **SATISFYING EXPERIENCE** than sitting amongst giggling tweens, spending $19 on a Pepsi and some Junior Mints, and having your feet gradually fuse to the sticky floor beneath you. Reading allows you to use this thing called your imagination. Seriously, how many times have you uttered something like, *I just can't picture Miley Cyrus in the role of Madame Bovary*? But there is one advantage to movie versions of books: They help sell books! If the movie version is so great, why does everyone run out and buy the book after seeing the movie? Think about it.

MOVIE VERSIONS OF BOOKS

Movies make all those complicated nuances and obscure allusions typical of books **EASIER TO DIGEST**. Plus, they are an awesome way to cram for that English final tomorrow morning. Hollywood does us the favor of casting attractive people in the leads, even if the role is a malnourished Slavic peasant with rickets. It's a basic human drive: We want to sit back and be entertained while gorging ourselves on preposterously sized **HIGH-FRUCTOSE-CORN-SYRUP-BASED TREATS**. Ever try consuming a giant tub of popcorn and an extra-large Cherry Coke while reading? It's logistically impossible. The butter makes the pages stick together. Not to mention that books appear to be going the same way as the dodo and the newspaper. Maybe if books had product placement and previews they could compete in the marketplace.

PABLO PICASSO

V

VINCENT VAN GOGH

★ WHO'S THE ★

GREATEST PAINTER OF ALL TIME?

PICASSO

Yes, Picasso was a misogynist lecher, and rumor has it that the artist even pleasured himself to his own work. All I can say is, "That's good painting, folks." Picasso **DECONSTRUCTED PAINTING**, sculpture, and the world around him and reassembled them to create a new vision. He mastered every genre, from social commentary to cubism. Van Gogh's swirly skies and yellow stars make for tasty Lucky Charms marshmallows, but Picasso fundamentally transformed art. To take another tack: When asked if someone is a good painter and the answer is no, you say, "He's no Picasso."

VAN GOGH

Van Gogh's genius and reputation have consistently appreciated in the years since his death, which testifies to the fact that he was way ahead of his time (while giving false hope to millions of untalented artists everywhere). The monetary value of his oeuvre will soon pass that of Picasso, whose reputation has essentially flatlined since the days when he painted his first deformed, three-breasted prostitute playing the viola next to a horse. Yes, Picasso had a series of dramatic affairs and a bizarre love/hatred for women, two qualities that are great for art, but come on, Van Gogh **CUT OFF HIS OWN EAR**. Now that's passion!

FURTHER DEBATE: Would You Rather . . .

Have your portrait painted by Picasso or Van Gogh?
Live in a world painted by Picasso or Van Gogh?
Have your child's guidance counselor be Picasso or Van Gogh?

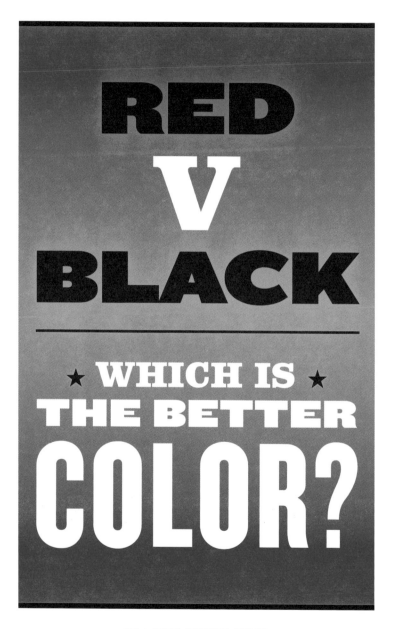

RED V BLACK

★ WHICH IS ★ THE BETTER COLOR?

RED

BLACK

POP QUIZ:
Which of the Following are Crayola Crayon Colors?

A. Timberwolf

B. Heather Heather

C. Gangreen

D. Mauvelous

E. Macaroni and Cheese

F. Pleasantly Puce

ANSWERS: a., d., and e.

ERNEST HEMINGWAY

V

NORMAN MAILER

WHO WAS THE BEST MACHO, DEPRESSED, SELF-DESTRUCTIVE AMERICAN WRITER ★ OF THE TWENTIETH CENTURY? ★

DIDN'T YOU KNOW? Fun Facts About Hemingway

- He was a boxer in his youth.
- He survived two plane crashes.
- He underwent electroshock therapy in 1961 to treat depression.

ERNEST HEMINGWAY

Winner of the Nobel and Pulitzer Prizes, Hemingway can out-write, out-drink, and out-brood Mailer any day. Hemingway's stories and novels exude the **TRAGIC WISDOM** of his experiences attained while driving an ambulance on the front in WWI, covering the Spanish Civil War, hunting on safari, and living in Paris, Key West, the Bahamas, and Idaho. Compare that to Mailer, who served as a cook in the military and spent most of his life in Brooklyn…Heights. Can one be awarded the Purple Heart for stacking cans of corn? *The Naked and the Dead* is to *For Whom the Bell Tolls* as Christian Slater is to Jack Nicholson. And by the way, Norm, there's nothing like a cameo on *Gilmore Girls* to preserve your artistic credibility.

NORMAN MAILER

Mailer's got nine kids with six different wives. That's NBA territory as far as volatile, drug-addled relationships go. And what is so brilliant about writing in short sentences and plain language? By that reasoning, there are about two million fifth graders penning "masterpieces" every day at school. The only difference is that their "My Summer Vacation" papers don't talk about bull-fighting, drunken self-destruction, and womanizing. Though Mailer may have spent most of his life in New York, he used his time wisely and started the formerly-hipper-than-thou *The Village Voice*. And, Ernie, check out this second **PULITZER PRIZE**. Oh, and try biting off part of Rip Torn's ear. Now that's Mailer.

VERDANA

V

TIMES
NEW ROMAN

WHICH IS THE

★ BETTER ★

FONT?

VERDANA

W eird Al Yankovic should write a song to the tune of Toto's "Rosanna" called "Verdana" about how great this font is. Verdana has ample space both between and within its characters, allowing them to breathe. Verdana is sans serif. "Serif" translates to those little spokes and flares on letters, and "sans," of course, translates to "too cool for." Plus, Verdana is a font of the times. It was created specifically for on-screen reading. It looks as good in 8 point as it does in 12 point. TNR is DNR, dead.

TIMES NEW ROMAN

S imple, functional, and respectful, Times New Roman is the undisputed king of fonts. Its serifs are not merely ornamental, mind you—they help the letters flow, leading the eye across the text during reading, which is not only efficient but also ensures that the eye doesn't get stuck in between letters. They also distinguish characters from one another more clearly. And, I don't buy this "Verdana is better for the screen" crap. Maybe in the Vic 20 days, serifs were a problem. But now, most modern computer monitors can display fonts with almost as much perceived clarity as a printed page, rendering a wussy font like Verdana basically obsolete.

FURTHER DEBATE:

Arial **v** Garamond?
ALGERIAN **v** Goudy Stout?
11 point **v** 12 point?

YO MOMMA

V

YO-YO MA

★ **WHO WOULD WIN IN A** ★

SNAPS BATTLE?

FUN FACTS: Yo Momma Jokes Throughout History

COLONIAL: Yo momma's head is so big,
she needs a four-cornered hat!

JAPANESE HAIKU: Yo momma expands
Filling air like morning fog
Infinite fat one

THE FUTURE: **INITIALIZE INSULT:** The cloning unit which
resulted in yo momma's creation is defective.
The defect has been identified as an excess
of body weight. **END INSULT.**

YO MOMMA

YO MOMMA IS SO FAT, she eats Wheat Thicks.

YO MOMMA IS SO STUPID, she trips over a cordless phone!

YO MOMMA IS SO UGLY, when she walks into a bank, they turn off the surveillance cameras.

YO MOMMA IS SO OLD, her social security number is 1!

YO MOMMA IS SO POOR, she eats cereal with a fork to save milk.

YO MOMMA IS SO SHORT, she models for trophies.

YO MOMMA IS SO NASTY, she makes Speed Stick slow down.

YO-YO MA

YO-YO MA IS SO STUPID, he took his cello in to get it fixed because they told him it was Baroque!

YO-YO MA'S TEETH ARE SO CROOKED, he can floss with his bow.

YO-YO MA IS SO OLD, he played live accompaniment for Schubert, fool!

YO-YO MA IS SO UGLY, he lives under his cello's bridge! Aw, damn!

YO-YO MA IS SO CRAZY, he eats "Crescend-os" for breakfast!

YO-YO MA IS SO LAME, his rap name is Trouble Clef.

DEBATE
AMONGST
YOURSELVES:
CULTURE
CLASHES

★ ★ ★ ★ ★ ★ ★ ★ ★ ★ ★ ★

UP 'TIL NOW, THE ARGUMENTS HAVE BEEN MADE FOR YOU. HERE'S YOUR CHANCE TO PUT YOUR DEBATE SKILLS TO WORK. FIND A WORTHY OPPONENT, CHOOSE YOUR SIDE, AND PREPARE FOR BATTLE—FREESTYLE. WHO WOULD WIN THESE DISCOURSES OF THE DISTINGUISHED?

Old Testament v *New Testament*

George Carlin v Richard Pryor

Jane Eyre v *Emma*

Calvin and Hobbes v Charlie Brown and Snoopy

Hermione Granger v Éowyn

The Grapes of Wrath v *The Great Gatsby*

Hans Christian Andersen v Lewis Carroll

Scrabble v Pictionary

"Dickensian" v "Kafkaesque"

Holden Caulfield v Boo Radley

Haikus v Limericks

Time v *Newsweek*

Oscar Wilde v David Sedaris

Duchamp's *Fountain* v Andy Warhol's *Campbell's Soup Cans*

Monet v Manet

Catch-22 v *Catch-22*

CHAPTER ★ TWO ★

SPORTS

&

LEISURE

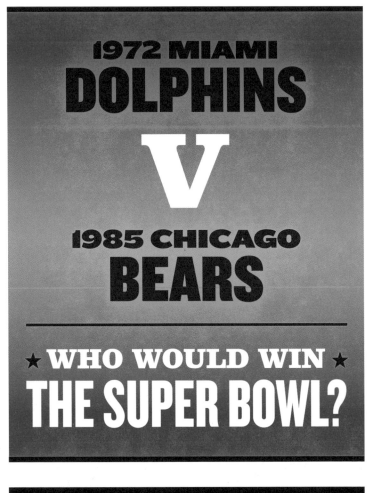

1972 MIAMI DOLPHINS

V

1985 CHICAGO BEARS

★ WHO WOULD WIN ★

THE SUPER BOWL?

POP QUIZ

What was the Bears's linebacker Mike Singletary's nickname?

ANSWER: Samurai Mike.

'72 DOLPHINS

The '72 Dolphins are the only team to go **UNDEFEATED FOR AN ENTIRE SEASON**. While the Bears may have dominated '85, so did acid-wash jeans. No fullback, before or since, has ever been as tough as Larry Csonka, the man with the best name not just in sports, but in anything ever. *Csonka*. It's onomatopoetic. Not that the Bears would know what that meant. But supergenius coach Don Shula would. Cool as a dolphin's skin, Shula's hard-nosed running game would have given Mike Ditka a heart attack by the second quarter. Along with Shula, six players from the '72 Dolphins team are enshrined in the Pro Football Hall of Fame. Whatever happened to Jim McMahon and the rest of the Shufflin' Crew anyways? Last we heard, the Fridge was on *Celebrity Boxing* getting trounced by Manute Bol.

'85 BEARS *

Paradoxically, the Bears were **SO BAD, THEY KNEW THEY WERE GOOD**. Furthermore, they absolutely blew your mind, as they were well aware they would. They did not perform with the objective of starting no trouble. On the contrary, they had one primary near-rhyming motive: to simply do the Super Bowl Shuffle. Armed with greats like Walter "Sweetness" Payton, William "The Refrigerator" Perry, and Jim "The Punky Q.B." McMahon, the Bears were not, despite certain accusations, doing this to be greedy. In fact, they were doing it for the antithetical reason of feeding the needy. Bottom line: the Bears were more than anything else a shuffling crew, and moreover, they were doing it for you.

* This entry is attributed to the "Super Bowl Shuffle."

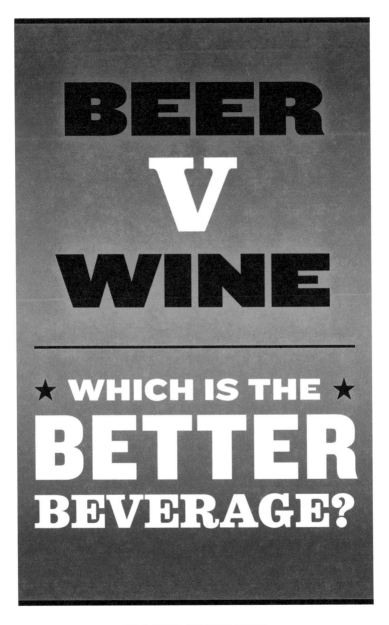

BEER
V
WINE

★ WHICH IS THE ★
BETTER
BEVERAGE?

BEER

Dude! Word up? Did you see the USC/LSU game? Sick. Anyway, brah, you know I'm the best. What could be better than hanging with some brosiffs, downing a few cold ones, listening to the new Dave, and getting ready to lay down some serious game on some Betties? (Fistbump.) I'll lay it out for you like I did to that glass of Pinot Noir that was giving me crap: **I QUENCH YOUR THIRST, I DROWN YOUR SORROWS, AND I GIVE YOU FALSE CONFIDENCE**—(imitating Dick Vitale) *the trifecta, baby!* I mean, what are you gonna do, grab a bottle of Sauvignon Blanc to watch the Bears game? Here, have another one on me.

WINE

Good evening. If I may . . . I am not merely a conduit to stupor, but **A VITAL PART OF ANY GOURMET CULINARY EXPERIENCE**. I complement with nuance that which one consumes. I excite the palate, even when I am the only instrument in a gustatory sonata. Moreover, my antioxidant composition— resveratrol, polyphenols, and proanthocyanidins—has been proved by scientists to improve your health and longevity. Historically, I am the drink of kings and the beverage of ritual. Beer is a beverage best fit for . . . how shall I say it? Peasants. After all, Jesus did not turn water into Coors Light (self-amused chuckle).

FURTHER DEBATE:
Which Goes Better with the Following Meals, Beer or Wine?

- Pizza? • London broil? • Seasoned tilapia?
- A bowl of Fruit Loops after you just got fired and your spouse leaves you? • Your last meal?

COOKIE MONSTER

V

PAC-MAN

★ WHO WOULD WIN IN A ★
COMPETITIVE-EATING
CONTEST?

WILDCARD:
Excerpt from *Pac-Man: The Unauthorized Biography*

Ever-chomping, Pac-Man fled, his mind a blur of dots and darkness. He was operating on instinct now, navigating the labyrinthine hell with a madness to match the situation. Blinky pursued, undead and pastel, the blank look in his eyes belying his thirst for death. And then, in an instant, it all changed. Night was day. Light was dark. For the gluttonous refugee had reached his engorged spheroid goal, and just like that, the chaser had become the chasee.

COOKIE MONSTER

Cookie Monster is a deeply sick individual, but the puppet can eat. And we're talking about the original CM, not the cleaned-up, post-rehab CM who shuns bad eating habits after over-concerned educators revamped *Sesame Street*. (Were they afraid that the letter "R" was going to pull its sponsorship?) He is **A NATURAL GLUTTON**, pathologically insatiable. And while we've mainly seen him eat cookies, there's no reason to suspect he could not tailor his habit to other foods. Pac-Man may be a strong eater, but if the spontaneously appearing fruit is any indication, the guy's about the size of a softball, and that's if we give him a generous three-dimensional interpretation. There is only so much space for all those pellets and fruit to go, even with the aid of a preemptive black tea–induced colon cleansing.

PAC-MAN

Pac-Man **WILL EAT ANYTHING**. Pellets, ghosts, cherries, pretzels, oranges, peaches—anything. The maniac will even eat a *key*. That's not even *food*. Put it in front of him and watch him go at it. The little guy literally needs food to move forward. He eats like we mere mortals breathe. If he were to stop eating, it would be like a shark that stops swimming (i.e., a dead Pac-Man). Defying intestinal logic, he can take down hundreds of pellets and still have room left for Blinky and Clyde. As for Cookie Monster, we'd advise the judges to pay close attention. The cheater rarely actually swallows, he just pulverizes food and lets it fall from his mouth. Pac-Man wins by DQ.

MUHAMMAD ALI

V

MIKE TYSON

★ **WHO WOULD WIN A** ★
"TANGLE IN TIME-SPACE"
IN HIS PRIME?

POP QUIZ: What'd He Just Say?

CAN YOU REPLACE THE INCORRECT WORD (IN ITALICS) IN EACH
MIKE TYSON QUOTE WITH THE CORRECT ONE?

- **A.** "I might just fade into *bolivian*, you know what I mean?"

- **B.** "I'm not going to make a *skeptical* out of my career."

- **C.** "I really dig Hannibal. Hannibal had real guts. He rode
  elephants into *Cartilage*."

ANSWERS: a. oblivion, b. spectacle, c. Carthage

MUHAMMAD ALI

(56 WINS, 5 LOSSES, 37 KNOCKOUTS)

Ali said it best: He floats like a butterfly and stings like a bee. And that's one seriously dangerous insect hybrid. No one has ever displayed the **SKILL AND TIMING** that Ali had in his prime, nor the **INTELLIGENCE**. Tyson would be an all-too-willing dope in Ali's rope-a-dope ring psychology. Let's break it down. Ali's got a **LONGER REACH** (80 inches to Tyson's 71) and has the edge in **SPEED** and **AGILITY**. Ali has a history of withstanding and defeating hard-punchers: Foreman, Liston, Frazier, Norton, Shavers—the list goes on. Last point of comparison: Ali is a masterful **POET**. Tyson is a poet only in the Eddie Murphy "Kill My Landlord" sense. Ali by T.K.O. in the ninth.

MIKE TYSON

(50 WINS, 6 LOSSES, 2 NO CONTESTS, 44 KNOCKOUTS)

Tyson doesn't need "distractions" like speed, grace, and intelligence. What he's got over Ali is **POWER** and **ANGER**. And that's really all he needs to **CRUSH** any opponent, not unlike the way he used to crush pigeons with his bare hands during his juvenile delinquent days. Tyson's just **TOUGHER**, period. Tyson-like power didn't even exist in Ali's day. In fact, last time I checked, poetry was not exactly a "tough guy" hobby. But let's forget his ridiculous **STRENGTH**, and talk about his other advantage: **INSANITY**. If the match lasts, Ali would prevail. Too bad it won't. Tyson by K.O. in the sixth.

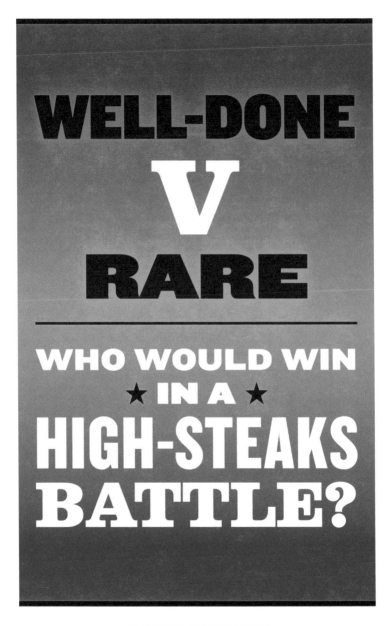

WELL-DONE

Well-done is the **CLASSY** and **EVOLVED** order. After all, we are not cavemen fleeing from sabre-toothed tigers. We take time to cook our meals. We marinate, we garnish, we use forks and knives, and we chew with our mouths closed. Rare steak appeals to meatheads; it's the daily fare at a table of Pat Buchanans. And do not knock preparing your food responsibly. When well-done steak eaters are still at the dinner table enjoying a second helping of crème brûlée, their rare counterparts will be hunched in pain over a toilet, their digestive tract a playground of parasites and E. coli.

RARE

Rare appeals to our basic instincts. Like it or not, we are carnivores. There is a deeply **PRIMITIVE PLEASURE** in tearing into a red, sinewy piece of animal flesh and letting the juices run down our chins in a liquid medley of blood, saliva, and A-1 sauce. Plus, the **JUICIER** the meat, the **TASTIER**. Well-done is for cowards. It's the safe pick, the well-groomed preppie to rare's rebellious greaser. Just look at the linguistic connotations. "Rare" means "special" and "uncommon," as in rare gems, rare forms, and rare birds. "Well-done" is the mild compliment of a dowdy Brit, as in "well-done, old chap." Steak dries as it is overcooked, and with it dries the soul of the eater.

FURTHER DEBATE: Which is the Best Side Dish?

Creamed Spinach
Baked Potato with Sour Cream and Butter
French Fried Potatoes
Lobster

SUMMER GAMES

V

WINTER GAMES

WHICH IS THE
★ BETTER ★
OLYMPICS?

FURTHER DEBATE:
Which Events Would Be Included in an "Autumn Olympics"?

- Apple-bobbing
- Speed-raking
- Power-raking
- Synchronized harvesting
- Full-contact cider-mulling
- Triathlon: Pumpkin-smashing, pie-making, pie-throwing for accuracy/hilarity

SUMMER GAMES

How many ways can you go down a hill? One ski, two skis, through flags, not through flags, sitting in a sled, lying down in a sled. We get it. Just look at the absurdity of some of the signature events: the biathlon, with its combination of **SKIING AND SHOOTING**? Does this stem from some sort of European secret agent training? (Note: Secret Agent Games would be awesome.) What's next? Speed skating and archery? Snowshoeing and knitting? Luge and tanning? The real thrill of watching the Winter Games comes from seeing some poor ski jumper do a massive face plant or a triple-axeling figure skater **BITE ICE**. It's pure schadenfreude (which is why Germany has always fared well).

WINTER GAMES

How many ways can you swim across a pool? Backstroke, breaststroke, butterfly, doggie paddle. Surely one **SWIMMING EVENT** would be enough? Just get to the other end of the pool as fast as you can. At least with snow sports, you use different equipment. And what's going on with "sports" like synchronized swimming, trampoline, and rhythmic gymnastics? What's next: competitive parading? How about battle haiku? In the winter, we could really use the **ENTERTAINMENT**; but in the summer, we should all be enjoying the outdoors the way it was meant to be enjoyed—with some sun, surf, and waterskiing/shooting.

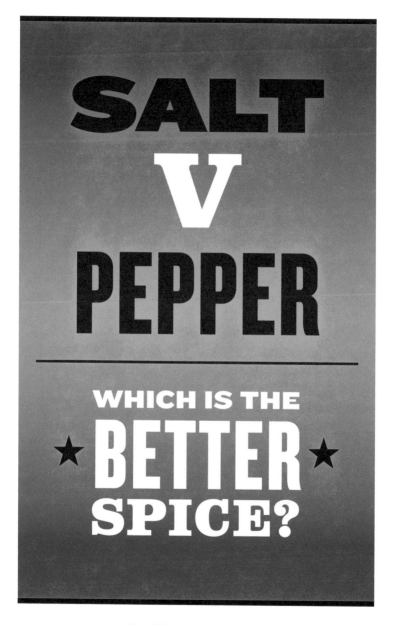

SALT

V

PEPPER

WHICH IS THE
★ BETTER ★
SPICE?

SALT

There's a reason the phrase is "salt and pepper" and not the other way around. Salty is **ONE OF THE FIVE BASIC TASTES**. Salt is the ultimate flavor enhancer, the one spice the cook cannot do without. Peppery? Doesn't even rank. Salt never gets old. In fact, salt **KEEPS OTHER THINGS FROM SPOILING**. Fresh pepper is nice, if you don't mind going shopping for fresh peppercorns. Pepper is a sidekick—the wacky neighbor, the quirky-but-ultimately undesirable best friend to salt's leading man. And by the way, could less pepper come out from a typical shake? It takes half an hour to dust scrambled eggs. Ridiculous.

PEPPER

Say what you will about pepper's status, there's no documented study citing pepper's health hazards. **SALT KILLS!** It's about time pepper bailed on this unhealthy relationship. There are other flavors out there that will appreciate pepper, corns and all. **TWO WORDS: LEMON PEPPER**. Oh, and, salt, thanks for making the majority of Earth's water undrinkable. You don't see any pepper water, do you? (Note to self: Pitch pepper water to Evian.)

DIDN'T YOU KNOW?

The fifth taste is called *umami*, which is a complex taste translated from the Japanese as "savory." Umami is found in ample amounts in Parmesan cheese, soy sauce, meats, mushrooms, and chicken broth.

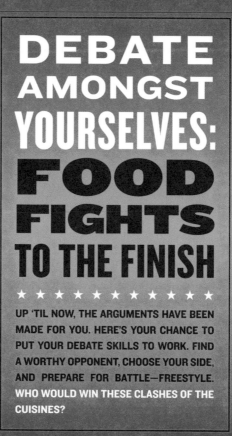

DEBATE AMONGST YOURSELVES: FOOD FIGHTS TO THE FINISH

★ ★ ★ ★ ★ ★ ★ ★ ★ ★ ★

UP 'TIL NOW, THE ARGUMENTS HAVE BEEN MADE FOR YOU. HERE'S YOUR CHANCE TO PUT YOUR DEBATE SKILLS TO WORK. FIND A WORTHY OPPONENT, CHOOSE YOUR SIDE, AND PREPARE FOR BATTLE—FREESTYLE. WHO WOULD WIN THESE CLASHES OF THE CUISINES?

Pancakes v Waffles

Dr. Atkins v Jennie Craig

Chocolate v Vanilla

Tap water v Perrier

Julia Child v Martha Stewart

Red wine v White wine

Skim milk v Whole milk

Yogurt commercials v Soup commercials

Rice v Prunes

Soup v Salad

Fries v Baked potatoes

Tums v Beano

Fig Newtons v Fig Newmans

Tofu v Nothing

THE EASTER BUNNY

V

SANTA CLAUS

WHO IS THE
★ BETTER HOLIDAY ★
ICON?

WILDCARD: Forgotten Holiday Icons

LORD OF BRISKET: He fills children's shoes with brisket every Rosh Hashanah.

FERN FRANKLIN: The Arbor Day tree who recites bawdy limericks.

GOBBLES THE EVIL TURKEY: An evil turkey who helps children nationwide rationalize the mass killing and eating of a species.

THE EASTER BUNNY

Santa Claus's day has come and gone. E-commerce sites like Amazon offer overnight delivery, rendering Santa's sled-and-reindeer distribution system hopelessly outdated. And the jolly fat man continues to be dogged by persistent ethics questions. Charges have been leveled about sweatshop-like working conditions in the Workshop, PETA is in an uproar about the treatment of his reindeer, and religious groups have hinted that his Christmas Eve ubiquity is a sign of **DARK MAGIC**. Let's face it: Santa is **OLD**, **OVERWEIGHT**, and probably diabetic after years of compulsive cookie consumption. And has he ever heard of email? Sheesh.

SANTA CLAUS

Is there anything more frightening than a giant humanoid bunny carrying a basket of eggs? I mean, it's the stuff of *Donnie Darko*–style nightmares. (And incidentally, which misguided church focus group picked the ever-breeding rabbit as the official Easter mascot?) Easter, with its abundance of chocolate bunnies, Cadbury Crème Eggs, and Peeps, not only contributes to the childhood obesity epidemic, but also necessitates the work of another dubious entity: the Tooth Fairy. (What kind of debauched nymph gets off on collecting the bloody teeth of little children?) As far as pagan figures go, **STICK WITH THE FAT MAN**.

BJÖRN BORG

V

ANDRE AGASSI

★ **WHO WOULD WIN** ★

IN A CLASH

ON THE COURT?

FURTHER DEBATE: Whose 'Do is Better?

Dr. J's afro v Michael Jordan's shaved head?

Dorothy Hamill's wedge v Tonya Harding's bangs?

Larry Bird's curly mullet v Troy Polamalu's long curls?

BJÖRN BORG

Borg won a staggering 89.8 percent of the Grand Slam singles matches he played. His playing style is the perfect foil to Agassi's. He can match him in **GROUNDSTROKES**, and his preternatural **ENDURANCE** would allow him to run down any and all of Agassi's balls. But let's get to the most interesting part of this matchup: hair. Borg's **HAIR WAS TIMELESS AND TASTEFUL**. Even in his fifties, he still has great hair. Agassi's frosted mullet-mane was a travesty and serves as a metaphor for his career: flashy. And by the way, who was Agassi's agent on that girlfriend/wife trade-in? Brooke Shields for Steffi Graf? In love, hair, and tennis, resistance against Borg is futile. Match: Borg.

ANDRE AGASSI

Agassi is the only tennis player to **WIN EVERY GRAND SLAM**, the Tennis Masters Cup, the Davis Cup, *and* an Olympic gold medal. He is probably the **BEST SERVE RETURNER** in the history of the game, and his groundstrokes instilled fear for their **PUNISHING ANGLES** and **POWER**. A matchup between Agassi and Borg would see Agassi in total control, running Borg all around the court until he reaches the point of headband sweat saturation (HSS). And check this out: Agassi's foundation has raised about 60 million dollars for at-risk youth in Nevada. See, it's not all about the hair. To whom do the proceeds of your underwear sales go, Björn? Match: Agassi.

APPLES
V
ORANGES

★ WHICH ARE ★
THE BETTER
FRUIT?

APPLES

TASTY. CRUNCHY. And that whole "apple a day keeps the doctor away" thing? Not just rhetoric. Research shows that apples reduce the risk of cancer, lower cholesterol, promote weight loss, and make for delicious pie fillings. They're high in vitamins, minerals, and amino acids, and have on average forty-seven calories. But all of that is second fiddle to the fact that you can enjoy them without needing a napkin. How's that orange you're eating? Oh, you're still peeling it? Let me know when you get to the fruit part and we can compare. Still peeling? That's cool. Are your hands getting sticky yet?

ORANGES

JUICY. REFRESHING. Oranges just taste better. Plus, one orange contains 12.5 percent of your recommended daily fiber and loads of antioxidants, potassium, vitamin C, folic acid (for the brain), and thiamin (for energy). They also help prevent everything from diabetes to kidney stones. You can no more easily match up against an orange as you can rhyme with it. Let's face it, eating an apple is a chore. It's inherently unsatisfying because you can never really finish it, and you never know when exactly to stop eating and what to do with the remaining part. How's that apple treating you? Not sure where to throw away that core? Sorry, can't help you with that one.

WILDCARD: Blueberries

The blueberry is considered by nutritionists to be a "superfood." It's at the top of the fruit chain in terms of antioxidants and said to fight aging and disease, as well as urinary infections, and it aids digestion, blood vessel strength, and vision.

HULK HOGAN

V

THE ROCK

WHO IS THE BEST
PRO WRESTLER
★ **OF ALL TIME?** ★

FURTHER DEBATE: Who Has the Better Catchphrase?

"Whatcha gonna do when Hulkamania runs wild on you?"

"Do you smell what The Rock is cooking?"

HULK HOGAN

Hogan and his "twenty-four-inch pythons" paved the way for a generation of imitators. He electrified massive crowds with his **DAZZLING ORATORY**, ushering in a new age wherein professional wrestlers replaced politicians as our nation's great rhetoricians. Hogan's **SUPERIOR CHARISMA** made a sidekick out of no less than Mr. T at Wrestlemania I. Anything The Rock has accomplished in his career was done while standing on Hogan's massively developed shoulders. Just try to find an example of communal elation as widespread as the day in Madison Square Garden when the Hulkster beat the Iron Sheik for the 1984 WWF **HEAVYWEIGHT** Championship. The Berlin Wall coming down paled in comparison to the moment that ref's hand hit the canvas. "1 . . . 2 . . . 3!"

THE ROCK

The Rock, unlike Hogan, is a **LEGITIMATE ATHLETE**, having played college football for the University of Miami Hurricanes. His athleticism was always on display in the ring, whether he was flying through the air or performing complicated maneuvers like the **ROCK BOTTOM**. Hogan, by contrast, could barely lumber from one end of the ring to the other. His signature move was the leg drop! That's right, the best he had to offer essentially involved sitting down on someone. The Rock Bottom, by contrast, required timing, **STRENGTH**, and a level of athleticism that only The Rock could muster. The Rock also had the good sense to shave his head when his hairline began to recede, while Hogan lets a single hair on the back of his neck grow long like decorative fringe. The result is just embarrassing—not unlike his reality show.

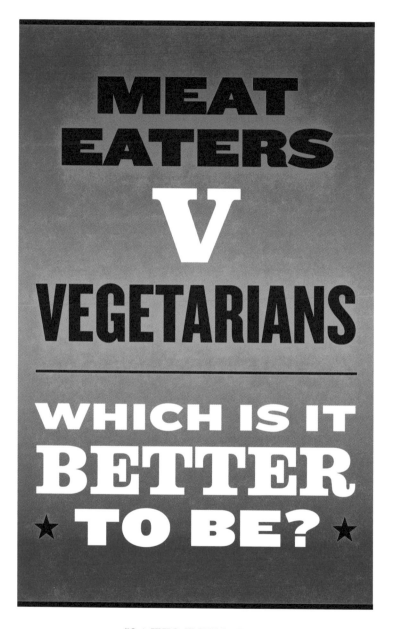

MEAT
EATERS
V
VEGETARIANS

WHICH IS IT
BETTER
★ TO BE? ★

MEAT EATERS

Eat meat for the sake of the cows. The majority of cows are bred for the express purpose of **PROVIDING MEAT** for human consumption. If you don't buy, ranchers will have no need to breed, and the cattle population will plummet—and the last thing we need is a longer endangered species list. Double your good-deed quotient by choosing meat raised on **SMALL FARMS** that eschew antibiotics and hormones, and instead use humane farming techniques to raise healthy cows. The ethical choice is to create the demand that encourages the fruitful multiplying of healthy animals (albeit so they may someday die).

VEGETARIANS

Vegetarianism is the obvious ethical position. Years from now, when meat is grown in petri dishes, we'll look back at our senseless **SLAUGHTER** of millions of **DEFENSELESS ANIMALS** and gasp with broccoli breath. But if ethics aren't enough for you, consider that much of the "meat" we eat contains other parts, including tail, head, feet, and rectum. Meat also contributes to your **FAT CONSUMPTION** and likelihood of developing heart disease. Want more reasons to go veggie? Most food poisoning is caused by meat, and if we ate the plants we currently feed to animals, the world's food shortage would end.

DIDN'T YOU KNOW? There's a Solution!

Douglas Adams in his *Hitchhiker's Guide to the Galaxy* series provided a middle ground to this debate. His answer: A line of cattle that loves to be slaughtered and takes pride in providing sustenance for humans.

THE BOSTON CELTICS

V

THE LA LAKERS

★ WHO WOULD WIN ★
IN AN ALL-TIME MATCHUP?

POP QUIZ:
Who Was the Least Attractive Boston Celtic of the '80s?

A. Larry Bird

B. Kevin McHale

C. Dennis Johnson

D. Robert Parish

ANSWER: e. All of the above.

BOSTON CELTICS

STARTERS: *Bob Cousy (PG), John Havlicek (SG), Larry Bird (SF), Kevin Garnett (PF), Bill Russell (C)*

BENCH: *Dennis Johnson, Jo Jo White, Kevin McHale, Sam Jones, Tom Heinsohn, Dave Cowens, Robert Parish*

According to statistical programs run by sports nerds, the Celtics would win this matchup 61.5 percent of the time. But stats aren't everything. The Celtics have always thrived on **TEAM UNITY**, and this is sure to transcend generations. The Lakers, on the other hand, can never get along. You think George Mikan is going to put up with **KOBE'S CRAP**? While Shaq and Kobe concern themselves with insulting each other through battle-rap, Cousy will be hitting Garnett on the break again and again.

LA LAKERS

STARTERS: *Magic Johnson (PG), Jerry West (SG), Kobe Bryant (SF), Elgin Baylor (PF), Kareem Abdul-Jabbar (C)*

BENCH: *Gail Goodrich, Michael Cooper, Byron Scott, James Worthy, George Mikan, Shaquille O'Neal*

Clearly, the Lakers have the advantage in the backcourt, where **MAGIC** would run the show. Playing Kobe at small forward would allow Jerry West to take the shooting guard position. Remember, any statistical breakdown does not factor in the three-point line for the older players. West would be a major three-point threat. Playing Elgin Baylor at power forward leaves the not-unwelcome dilemma of whether to start **SHAQ** or **KAREEM AT CENTER**. Either way, the combination would be too much for Russell and Parish to handle on the boards.

DEBATE
AMONGST
YOURSELVES:
FACE-OFFS
ACROSS
TIME

★ ★ ★ ★ ★ ★ ★ ★ ★ ★ ★ ★

UP 'TIL NOW, THE ARGUMENTS HAVE BEEN MADE FOR YOU. HERE'S YOUR CHANCE TO PUT YOUR DEBATE SKILLS TO WORK. FIND A WORTHY OPPONENT, CHOOSE YOUR SIDE, AND PREPARE FOR BATTLE—FREESTYLE. WHO WOULD WIN THESE SPATS OF THE SPORTS STARS?

Dr. J v Kobe Bryant

Jack Nicklaus v Tiger Woods

Martina Navratilova v Serena Williams

Brooklyn Dodgers v Los Angeles Dodgers

John Wooden v Coach K

1986–87 Lakers v 2001–02 Lakers

Sugar Ray Robinson v Sugar Ray Leonard

1975 Cincinnati Reds v 1998 New York Yankees

Mark Spitz v Michael Phelps

Shaq v Kareem

The Phoenix Suns Gorilla v The San Diego Chicken

Wayne Gretzky v Gordie Howe

Howard Cosell v John Madden

HOT DOG V HAMBURGER

★ WHAT IS THE MOST ★
QUINTESSENTIALLY AMERICAN FOOD?

HOT DOG

The hot dog is the symbol of America. Put the hot dog up against apple pie, and then we can have a civilized discussion—but the hamburger? Please. The hot dog is the epitome of American **INGENUITY** in that an existing tradition (in this case, the frankfurter) has been altered, renamed, and mass produced. It is the perfect food for a baseball game or a family picnic. Kind of hungry? Have one. Really hungry? Have two. Starving and insane? Enter Nathan's Hot Dog–Eating Contest. One final point: A hot dog is a **ONE-HANDED FOOD**, leaving your other hand available for other all-American activities, like drinking beer or scratching your crotch.

HAMBURGER

Nothing says "America" more than its fast-food restaurants. And nothing says "fast food" more than the good ol' hamburger (albeit a hamburger with a paper-thin patty that merely serves as a utensil for scooping up onion bits, ketchup, and corrugated pickles). A mound of **GROUND BEEF** on the grill is the beating heart of American barbecues. The foundation of the hamburger is strong: It is 100 percent(ish) ground beef. **GOD ONLY KNOWS WHAT'S IN A HOT DOG.**

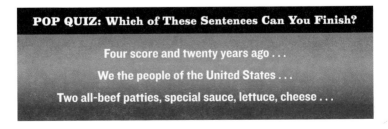

POP QUIZ: Which of These Sentences Can You Finish?

Four score and twenty years ago . . .

We the people of the United States . . .

Two all-beef patties, special sauce, lettuce, cheese . . .

TEA

Let's trust the children on this one: Children have "tea parties"; they don't play "barista." Tea is **MEDITATIVE**, medicinal, and even magical. It's rich in **ANTIOXIDANTS** that have been found to prevent cancer, prolong your lifespan, lower blood pressure, and fight the flu. Coffee is a tantrum in a cup. It fosters hyper-intense workaholism and turns us into jittery squirrels. It deprives us of the sleep we need with a false promise of short-lived energy, only to leave us weak and exhausted. It has turned us into addicts, and the pushers push our addictions from tall to grande to venti.

COFFEE

Tea-totalers, wake up and smell the you-know-what. Coffee is the lifeblood of our working class. It tastes great and increases **ALERTNESS** and mental acuity. Study after study proves that coffee in moderate amounts is actually good for our health; it is the dominant source of **ANTIOXIDANTS** for many of us. Coffee even helps ward off dementia. And it's time to blow the whistle on the whole "wellness beverage" scam the tea world has embraced with their misleading names like "calm" and "refresh." Tea is a sack of leaves, nothing more.

WILDCARD: Uninspiring Tea Flavors

DisappointMint

Cinnacism

Melon-choly

Berry, Berry Sad

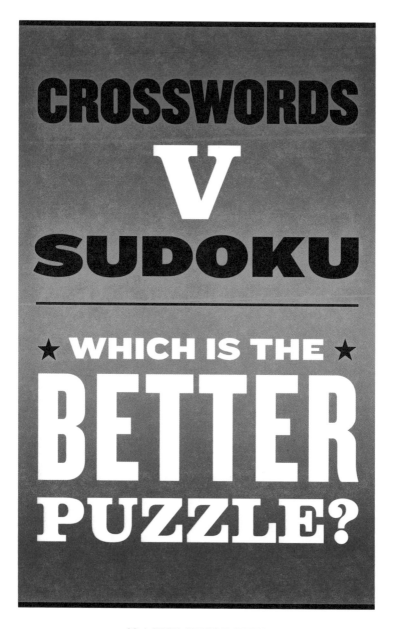

CROSSWORDS

Crosswords are the snowflakes of the puzzle world: They are exciting, **DELICATE**, and **BEAUTIFUL**, and no two are identical. Sudoku is the same thing every time. Maybe a "7" goes top left instead of bottom right. Big deal. They're artless, idle diversions that are barely better than the Jumble. So artless, in fact, that computers can create them. Crosswords, by contrast, must be painstakingly created by expert cruciverbalists. Ever try and make one up? I tried once, and just ended up with random letter combos, which I tried to pass off with clues like "potential Batman onomatopoeia" or "sound of a door hitting you in the face."

SUDOKU

Sudoku puzzles are mathematical absolutes. They require nothing more than the ability to count to nine, yet they hone the brain's **LOGIC** and **DEDUCTION SKILLS** and lead to infinite possibilities. Crossword puzzles, by contrast, have fundamental design flaws. Not only are their clues subjective and their symmetry imperfect, they require arcane knowledge of vowel-heavy milk products and Hawaiian instruments that you would never in a million years use in any conversation.

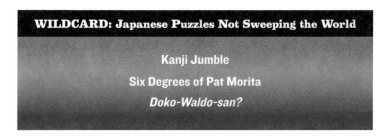

WILDCARD: Japanese Puzzles Not Sweeping the World

Kanji Jumble

Six Degrees of Pat Morita

Doko-Waldo-san?

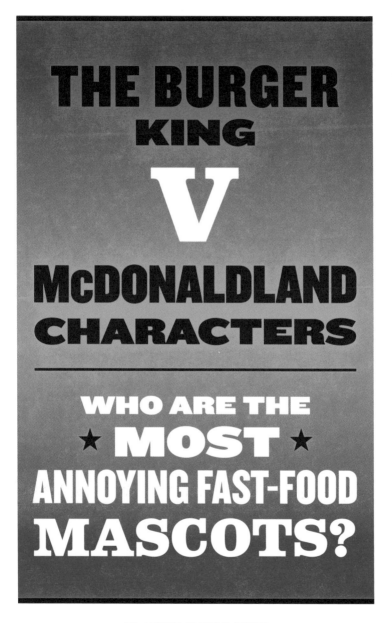

THE BURGER KING

V

McDONALDLAND CHARACTERS

WHO ARE THE ★ MOST ★ ANNOYING FAST-FOOD MASCOTS?

THE BURGER KING

BK finally landed a mascot for the ages when it reintroduced the King character in the early 2000s. The King is **STATELY BUT APPROACHABLE**, imaginary but realistic. A monarch of and for the people, he rules benevolently with Whoppers and shakes—when he's not starring in commercials that actually aren't that annoying. The same cannot be said for Ronald McDonald and the rest of the cracked-out citizens of McDonaldland. I mean, what the hell is Grimace? Ronald McDonald is a clown—simple enough. Mayor McCheese is a man with a cheeseburger for a face.

MCDONALDLAND CHARACTERS

Encouraging unhealthy eating habits in children for more than three decades, the McDonaldland characters are equally **COMFORTING AND ICONIC**. They are Bill Murray to the Burger King's Dane Cook. Less than a decade old, the King has already been overexposed. He and his perpetually eerie smile are the stuff of nightmares, a beast whose haunting visage will remain ingrained in children's psyches well into adulthood. He will fall the way of Bob's Big Boy, the Burger Chef, and all the other fast-food mascots who have kicked the KFC bucket.

FURTHER DEBATE:
Who Is the Creepier Fast-Food Mascot?

Taco Bell Chihuahua v Subway's Jared Fogle?
Domino's Noid v Rachael Ray of Dunkin' Donuts?
Colonel Sanders v Paris Hilton for Carl's Jr.?

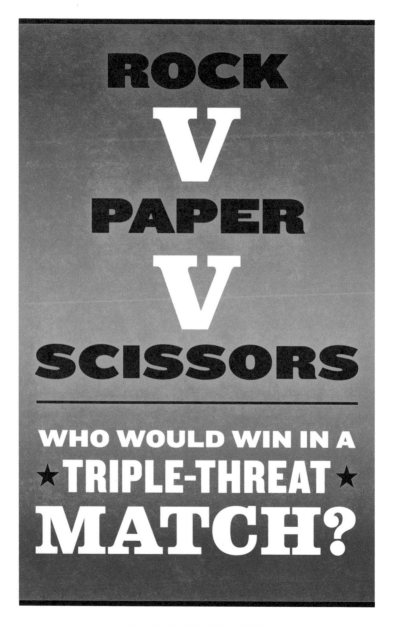

ROCK
V
PAPER
V
SCISSORS

WHO WOULD WIN IN A
★ TRIPLE-THREAT ★
MATCH?

ROCK

In a battle between Rock and Scissors, the edge clearly goes to Rock. The **HEAVINESS** and **HARDNESS** of Rock make it capable, with the right force applied, of bending, misshaping, even possibly breaking Scissors, thereby rendering them unusable. Conversely, stabbing Rock will only induce self-harm to Scissors, similar to that just described. That said, Rock is at a disadvantage against Paper, depending on the type. A poorly constructed low-grade Paper would be ground to pulp by Rock, but a strong fibrous hybrid could withstand Rock's effort if laid flat on a table. And, given a chance, Paper could envelop Rock, negating the "rockness" of Rock.

PAPER

As just described, Paper fares surprisingly well in a one-on-one battle against Rock. However, against Scissors, it's just hopeless. Paper *could* attempt to **ENVELOP SCISSORS**, but Scissors would outmaneuver it with an opening-closing motion to poke and cut, until the inevitable slashing of Paper occurs.

SCISSORS

Well, the outlook is good against Paper (see Paper). But Rock is where the problems arise (see Rock).

WILDCARD: Who's the Real Winner?

Stapler and Hole Puncher, who are busy getting it on during all this nonsensical fighting.

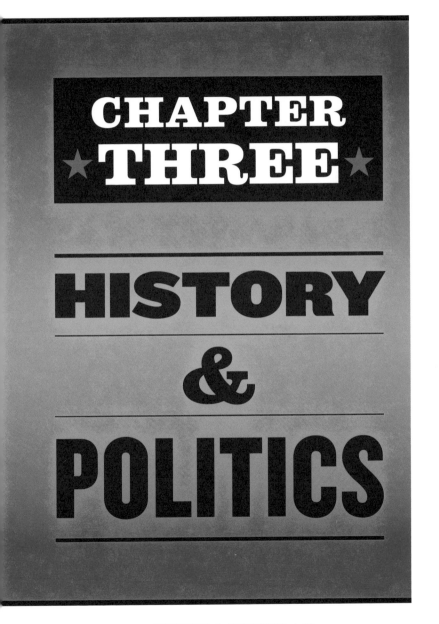

CHAPTER ★THREE★

HISTORY

&

POLITICS

GANDHI

V

MOTHER TERESA

★ WHO WOULD ★
WIN IN A
PEACE-OFF?

POP QUIZ: A Gandhi True or False

A. He had bad breath.

B. He had false teeth.

C. He had an Irish accent.

D. He was married at thirteen.

E. He liked to give reciprocal enemas and often greeted people by saying, "Have you had a good bowel movement this morning?"

ANSWERS: All are true.

GANDHI

Nobody comes close to Gandhi's quiet resolve, wisdom, and cool Lennon-esque specs. Gandhi **FREED** a people from the shackles of colonial oppression without resorting to violence. And he did it all on an empty stomach. Slim went without food for twenty-four days, and he fasted repeatedly in **NONVIOLENT PROTEST** against social and political injustices, including racism, colonialism, and the cruelties of India's caste system. Using his method of **CIVIL DISOBEDIENCE**, called Satyagraha (which means "truth and firmness" in Sanskrit), Gandhi led the 240-mile **SALT MARCH** to the city of Dandi in response to Britain's salt tax, which is ironic because the guy never ate a thing that required seasoning. If you serve up a relatively neat tofu sloppy joe, though, he might at least open negotiations.

MOTHER TERESA

Mother Teresa dedicated her entire life to helping the **POOR**. There was no one, **LEPERS INCLUDED**, her gentle hand would not touch. In 1950, she started the **MISSIONARIES OF CHARITY** to care for the poor and sick in Calcutta, and in 1965, the organization went **GLOBAL**. In 1982, she brokered a ceasefire between Israeli and Palestinian forces to rescue thirty-seven children from a hospital in Beirut. As for Gandhi, before he was peacemaker, the guy was a *lawyer*. Mother Teresa didn't need to take a year or two as an account manager in advertising before finding her true **LIFE'S PURPOSE**...at the age of twelve.

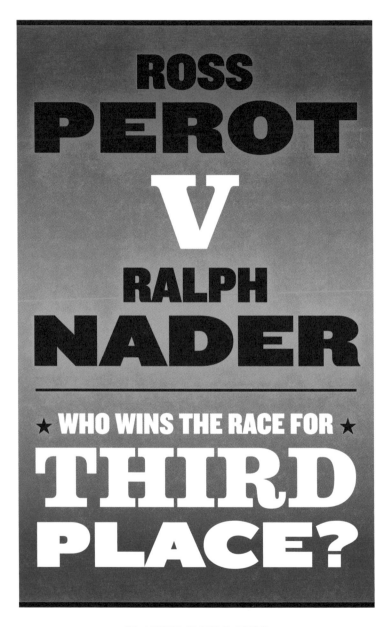

ROSS PEROT

Despite being a **TEXAN**, Perot offered progressive ideas. As a **BILLIONAIRE** CEO, his entrepreneurial spirit gave rise to perhaps his most important startup, the **REFORM PARTY**. While appealing to voters across the political spectrum, Perot paved the way for future mainstream party candidates by financing his own campaigns. Nader, by contrast, can't even afford decent campaign buttons. Add in a mumbling **ADMIRAL STOCKDALE** as a running mate, and the Perot ticket has a clear advantage when it comes to parody fodder, perhaps the single greatest contribution of third-party politics.

RALPH NADER

Nader is a much bigger loser than Perot, and with that argument he wins, hands down, in the contest for "best third place." In his never-ending quest for **THE BRONZE**, Nader even went with different parties, associating himself with the **GREEN PARTY** ticket and picking up the soiled remains of the Reform Party after Pat Buchanan tainted it. Not only do the vote tallies demonstrate that he is truly the most distant third, but also potentially the **MOST IMPACTFUL**. It's speculated that Nader's 97,488 votes contributed to Bush's victory in the 2000 race. Thanks, Ralphie.

FURTHER DEBATE

By extrapolation, who is more responsible for the Iraq War, Ralph Nader or Monica Lewinsky?

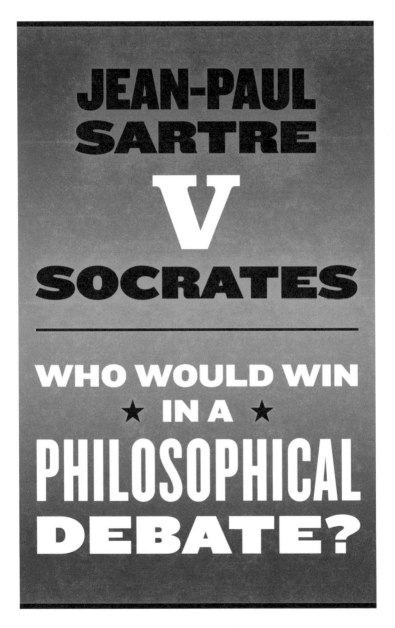

JEAN-PAUL SARTRE

V

SOCRATES

WHO WOULD WIN ★ IN A ★ PHILOSOPHICAL DEBATE?

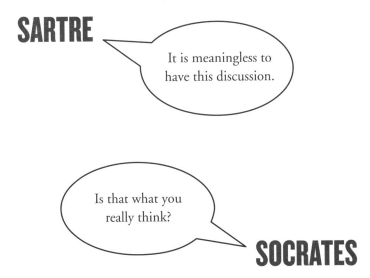

SARTRE

It is meaningless to
have this discussion.

Is that what you
really think?

SOCRATES

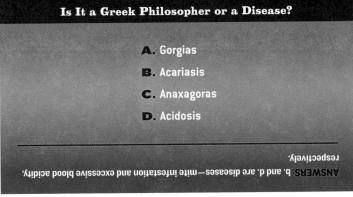

THIS OR THAT:
Is It a Greek Philosopher or a Disease?

A. Gorgias

B. Acariasis

C. Anaxagoras

D. Acidosis

ANSWERS: b, and d, are diseases—mite infestation and excessive blood acidity, respectively.

HAMMURABI
V
THE U.S.
FOUNDING FATHERS

★ WHO WAS THE BEST ★
LAWMAKER?

WILDCARD: How the Declaration of Independence Would Read If the Founding Fathers Played Mad Libs

When in the course of human farts, it becomes necessary for one poop to dissolve the political bands which have connected them with another and assume the buttheads of the earth, the separate and smelly station to which the Laws of Nature and Nature's washing machine entitle them, a decent respect to the opinions of dolphinkind requires that they should declare the double-farts which impel them to the rectum . . .

HAMMURABI

Answer this: *Hammurabi is*

a) a Jewish rapper
b) a fast-food chain mascot
c) a Babylonian king who wrote a bunch of really influential laws.

The answer is C. I challenge you to name one other person (besides Murphy) who still has laws named for him after nearly 4,000 years. **HAMMURABI'S CODE** of 282 laws include tenets that are still instituted around the world, including the presumption of innocence in criminal cases, the requirement of evidence, and the original **"EYE FOR AN EYE"** approach to punishment. Hammurabi claimed that he received them from the **SUN GOD SHAMASH**. If he could work side by side with gods, just imagine how effectively he must have worked across party lines (apparently Eshnunna was a red state in the 1760s B.C.E.).

THE U.S. FOUNDING FATHERS

More than 200 years after it was written by the Founding Fathers, the **CONSTITUTION** is the longest-surviving written charter of government. This is especially impressive given that it was written by a group of underdogs long before their nation became the world's dominant superpower. Hammurabi, by contrast, codified his laws toward the end of his rule, after he had already expanded his empire. Plus, his laws benefited from rather Draconian punishments (e.g., death) to ensure adherence. James Madison and the boys couldn't go this route, mainly because of the provision in the **8TH AMENDMENT** prohibiting cruel and unusual punishment. Thank goodness.

JIMMY CARTER

V

GEORGE W. BUSH

★ WHO WAS THE ★
WORSE
U.S. PRESIDENT?

POP QUIZ: Match the Quote to the Politician.

1. "I am mindful not only of preserving executive powers for myself, but for predecessors as well."

2. "At my age, any scream is a good scream."

3. "Republicans understand the importance of bondage between a mother and child."

A. Bill Clinton

B. Dan Quayle

C. George W. Bush

ANSWERS: 1. c., 2. a., 3. b.

JIMMY CARTER

How about some **MALAISE** with your **INFLATION** and high gas price sandwich? Mmm, tasty! People forget about the horrors of the Carter administration. It was a time so dismal and hopeless that the masses turned to Donna Summer and disco for relief. Carter's wimpiness not only prolonged the **IRAN HOSTAGE CRISIS**, but it enabled the tortuous popularity of one of the most insipidly catchy tunes in history, "Tie a Yellow Ribbon." Bush would have bombed the entire country and used yellow ribbons to tie up the body bags. And what kind of name is "Jimmy" for a president anyway? "Jimmy" is the kid with a paper route or the guy who sells you your lawn tractor, not president of the United States. Call yourself, James, farmer boy!

GEORGE W. BUSH

Every family has a black sheep: the Clintons have Roger; the Carters had Billy; and the Bushes have George W. Only in this case, the **BLACK SHEEP** was elected president. Bush hired a bunch of smurfs named Rummy, Brownie, Condie, and **CHENEY** to do all the work for him—and we all know how badly they smurfed things up. Carter was not only able to speak without a teleprompter, but his Camp David Accords showed that there *are* peaceful solutions to Middle East conflicts. Moreover, Carter munched discreetly on peanuts, Reagan on jelly beans, Clinton on hamburgers—all without difficulty. W.'s pretzel habit almost ended in death by salty treat. Bush can't even snack without inciting a **QUAGMIRE**.

CANADA V SWITZERLAND

★ WHO WOULD ★ WIN IN A WAR?

CANADA

(Elected to abstain from conflict)

SWITZERLAND

(Elected to abstain from conflict)

DIDN'T YOU KNOW?

The world's largest Swiss Army knife, designed by Wenger, has eighty-five tools, including a golf shoe spike wrench, a tire tread gauge, and a fish scaler.

DEBATE
AMONGST
YOURSELVES:
MILITARY
MATCHUPS
(ASSUMES EQUAL TROOPS, TECHNOLOGY, WEAPONRY, AND TRAINING)

★ ★ ★ ★ ★ ★ ★ ★ ★ ★ ★

UP 'TIL NOW, THE ARGUMENTS HAVE BEEN MADE FOR YOU. HERE'S YOUR CHANCE TO PUT YOUR DEBATE SKILLS TO WORK. FIND A WORTHY OPPONENT, CHOOSE YOUR SIDE, AND PREPARE FOR BATTLE—FREESTYLE. WHO WOULD WIN THESE BATTLES OF THE BRAWN?

Eisenhower v MacArthur

Napoleon v Rommel

General Powell v General Petraeus

Elizabeth I v "Bloody" Mary I

Sun Tzu v Leonidas of Sparta

Washington v Patton

Che Guevara v Joan of Arc

Julius Caesar v Bill Parcells

General Grant v General Bradley

Alexander the Great v Genghis Khan

Attila the Hun v Judas Maccabeus

General Robert E. Lee v General Grievous

SAMURAI V NINJA

WHO WOULD WIN A ★ JAPANESE ★ WARRIOR BRAWL?

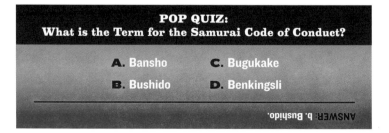

POP QUIZ:
What is the Term for the Samurai Code of Conduct?

A. Bansho **C.** Bugukake

B. Bushido **D.** Benkingsli

ANSWER: b. Bushido.

SAMURAI

Members of the Japanese military nobility, samurai are, above all, **HONORABLE**. So honorable, in fact, that if they fail in their legendary code of conduct or fall into enemy hands, they will publicly commit ritual suicide, called **SEPPUKU**. Samurai are team players, as represented by the term "shudo," which loosely translates to "unwavering borderline **HOMOEROTIC DEVOTION** to one another." Ninjas, by contrast, are sneaky assassins who wear their stealth like an undetectable badge of honor and live and die by "every man for himself." In any normal battle situation, samurai will prevail. In a forest, or maybe someplace backstage with lots of black curtains, it might be possible for a ninja to catch a samurai off guard. And, as weapons go, I don't know about you, but I'll take a samurai's katana, naginata, and wakizashi over a shobo, suntetsu, and ozutsu any day.

NINJA

Come on, there's **NOTHING COOLER** than a ninja. A ninja can kill you with this book. He can kill you with page 137 alone. In fact, he already has. The ink is laced with poison that reacts fatally with the oils in human skin. Samurai can gloat all they want about their honorable ways and parade around in their fancy outfits. You know what goes well with traditional samurai robes? A throwing star to the forehead. Set a ninja loose on a samurai and the ninja will have struck **PARALYZING** pressure points, unarmed him, picked his pocket, and altered his slacks before the samurai has a chance to say "hari-kiri." If the ninja's feeling magnanimous, maybe he'll let the humiliated samurai finish himself off in said ritual suicide. Sayonara, sucker.

GEORGE WASHINGTON

V

ABRAHAM LINCOLN

★ WHO WOULD WIN ★ IN A PRESIDENTIAL TRIATHLON?

FUN FACTS:
Coincidences About the Assassinations of Lincoln and Kennedy in Order of Decreasing Impressiveness:

- Lincoln had a secretary named Kennedy who told him not to go to the theater; Kennedy had a secretary named Lincoln who told him not to go to Dallas.

- Booth shot Lincoln in a theater and fled to a warehouse; Oswald shot Kennedy from a warehouse and fled to a theater.

- Both men's vice presidents were named Johnson and they were both southern Democrats and former senators.

- Neither man wore a feather boa when he was assassinated.

- Neither man had ever heard of string cheese.

DEBATE

WASHINGTON: No leader before or since rivals Washington's legendary charisma. Tall in stature and big in presence, Washington commands, period.

LINCOLN: Lincoln was the most eloquent of eloquent speakers. He was the anti-Bush. He'd make Douglas out of Washington in no time.

ONE-ON-ONE BASKETBALL

WASHINGTON: At 6'4" (6'5" with wig) Washington was a formidable athlete, as evidenced by his skill in the most popular sport of his day: war. He knew a good defense was vital to win.

LINCOLN: At 6'5" (6'10" with top hat) Lincoln also excelled at the most popular sports of his day: driving railroad spikes and splitting wood for respect. You'd be surprised how well railroad spike–driving translates to shot-blocking.

GETTING THE LADIES

WASHINGTON: Okay, Washington was no Kennedy, but he was no Lincoln either. Physically, it looks like Lincoln had the air sucked out of his head (and sorry, but that beard isn't hiding anything). Women like a man in uniform. March on, General.

LINCOLN: Lincoln has the whole sensitive brooding thing going on. He's like a wounded bird that needs fixing. The ladies love that.

THE '80s
V
THE '90s

WHICH WAS THE
★ BETTER ★
DECADE?

THE '80s

Make fun of the '80s all you want, but **BIG HAIR** and shoulder pads were emblematic of a society having a good time. The decade's hippie backlash saw a popular culture juiced up on **DECADENCE**: material girls, moonwalkers, Hypercolor T-shirts, and an upbeat drug du jour **(CRACK COCAINE)**. If the '80s were the party, the '90s were the hangover. How else can you explain a fashion trend that gives the illusion that we're all out-of-work carpenters? Moreover, the '90s lionized a genre of music that complained about the difficulties of being upper-middle class. Gag me with a spoon.

THE '90s

Contrary to what you might think, the '90s were **GOOD TIMES**. It only took a few years to dispel the **GEN-X** myth and propel the world (finally) into the technological future. The '90s spread the Internet, mobile **TECHNOLOGY**, and all the other things we now take for granted. What'd the '80s produce? Brick cell phones and Electronic Battleship? And, hey, is that a rat tail? That's gonna stick. Timeless, like a nice dark suit. You know how you can tell if a decade is ridiculous? If it becomes a popular theme at clubs and parties. You don't see a whole lot of '90s clubs.

WILDCARD: Key Cultural Touchstones by Decade

'80s: Rubik's Cube, *Cheers*, Cabbage Patch Kids, Wacky Wall-Walkers, Reasonable WallWalkers, *The A-Team*, Commodore 64, *Smurfs*, scratch-and-sniff stickers, indeterminable location of the beef

'90s: Grunge, birth of the Internet, *Teletubbies*, slackers, the Macarena, *Street Fighter*, Pogs, Zima, Beanie Babies, gangsta rap, SUVs, *Seinfeld*

CHAPTER FOUR ★

★

ENTERTAINMENT

★ ★ ★

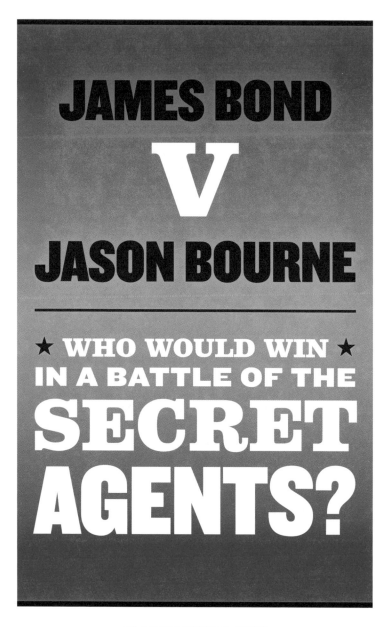

JAMES BOND

V

JASON BOURNE

★ WHO WOULD WIN ★
IN A BATTLE OF THE
SECRET
AGENTS?

JAMES BOND

From beverage ordering to assassination to unprotected sex, Bond handles everything with **EFFORTLESS APLOMB**. Bourne is so damn intense and angry about everything, he looks like he has stomach issues all the time. (Constipation is a severe hindrance in espionage.) Bond's also got a **HEIGHT ADVANTAGE**: While his exact measurements have varied over the years, he always comes in over 1.83 meters (that's six feet), compared with Bourne, who's lucky if he's a member of the 5'8"–5'9" club. On the road, Bond's Q-equipped **SPORTS CARS** would take Bourne down. Last time I checked, Mini Coopers don't have a missile option.

JASON BOURNE

Bourne is a secret agent for our times. Troubled and brooding, he's a **MAN OF SUBSTANCE** and moral ambiguity. He has mystique but still **KICKS ASS**. He is young and strong, and in hand-to-hand combat, he'll easily win (especially if we're talking about Roger Moore or Pierce Brosnan). Bond is an anachronism. And more importantly, he is gadget-reliant. Take away his inhaler/flamethrower or his boomerang/cell phone and he's just another English dude in an expensive suit. He's Maxwell Smart with VD. British cool is so eighteenth century. And are you *sure* Daniel Craig is over 1.83 meters?

FURTHER DEBATE

WHO IS THE BEST BOND? Connery, Moore, Dalton, Brosnan, or Craig?

WHO WOULD BE THE WORST BOND? Hugh Grant, Daniel Day-Lewis, John Cleese, or Anthony Hopkins (circa 1980)?

ACTORS TURNED
MUSICIANS

V

MUSICIANS TURNED
ACTORS

★ WHO IS MORE ★
HORRIBLE?

ACTORS TURNED **MUSICIANS**

You're probably thinking: If actors didn't become musicians, how else would we know that **EDDIE MURPHY'S** girl had a propensity to party all the time? The ramifications would be disastrous! And how would we get through lonely nights if not for **BRUCE WILLIS'S** thoughtful blues covers? Yes, sometimes an actor pulls off a decent musical performance, but it is rare. For every **JOHN BELUSHI**, there's a Jim Belushi. The key is not to take it too seriously (got that, Don Johnson?). So, movie stars, satisfy your insatiable need for attention the way you do best, by acting out.

MUSICIANS TURNED **ACTORS**

Singers make it because of their voices. Movie stars make it because of their looks. **BARBRA STREISAND** and **LYLE LOVETT** were simply not meant to have their faces magnified two hundred times. As if the wooden acting performances of pop stars from **MARIAH CAREY** to **STING** weren't bad enough, we have now been blessed with a new hyphenate, that wonderful class of auteur known as the "rapper-actor." And 50 Cent in *Get Rich or Die Tryin'*? I want my ten dollars and 50 cent back.

FURTHER DEBATE:
Which Hybrid Profession Would You Rather Have?

Toll booth attendant/therapist v Shoe salesman/pedicurist?
Taxi driver/spoken-word artist v House painter/performance artist?
Priest/game show host v Plumber/sous chef?

BRUCE SPRINGSTEEN

V

JON BON JOVI

★ WHO WOULD WIN ★
THE TUSSLE ON THE TURNPIKE?

POP QUIZ: It's Not About That

"BORN IN THE USA" IS OFTEN MISINTERPRETED AS A PATRIOTIC SONG. IF YOU ACTUALLY LISTEN TO THE LYRICS, YOU WILL REALIZE IT'S ABOUT A VIETNAM WAR VETERAN'S UNHAPPY RETURN TO THE STATES. WHICH OF THE FOLLOWING STATEMENTS ABOUT SONG LYRICS IS TRUE?

A. "Turning Japanese" by The Vapors is about World War II.

B. Billy Idol's "White Wedding" is an anti-marriage song.

C. "Centerfield" by John Fogerty is actually about committing suicide.

D. Aerosmith's "Janie's Got a Gun" is about a housewife making an omelet.

ANSWER: Idol has said "White Wedding" refers to his dislike for his sister's fiancé and his overall unfavorable view of marriage.

BRUCE SPRINGSTEEN

Who's **THE BOSS**? That's a rhetorical question, of course. Everyone knows it's Springsteen. By comparison, Jon Bon Jovi is rock 'n' roll's administrative assistant. Let's compare career highlights. Springsteen has **EIGHTEEN GRAMMYS**, while Bon Jovi has one (and it's for "Best Country Collaboration," which is actually a strike against him). The Boss oozes gravitas while playing benefit concerts for the likes of **AMNESTY INTERNATIONAL**. Bon Jovi oozes hair gel while playing Ally McBeal's love interest. Springsteen was the first-ballot inductee into the New Jersey Hall of Fame. Bon Jovi didn't even make the initial cut. Bon Jovi is clearly not "Born to Run."

JON BON JOVI

Bon Jovi is a **HIT MACHINE**. *Slippery When Wet* sold over twenty-six million copies! He has **KICKASS HAIR** and good looks, and ladies **LOVE THE WAY HE MOVES**. Springsteen can't touch Bon Jovi in the looks department (hell, he can't even touch Max Weinberg in that department). And as for the Boss's epileptic dancing? There's a reason he's doing it in the dark. His "Boss" moniker smacks of an irrepressible condescension. Thanks for the lecture about eradicating Third World hunger, now will you just shut up and play "Glory Days"? Face it, the majority of Springsteen's songs are bitter and depressing, no matter how many "nah-nah-nahs" he puts in them. Bruuuuuce is going down in a "Blaze of Glory."

X-MEN V JUSTICE LEAGUE

★ WHO WOULD WIN ★
IN A SUPERHERO BATTLE ROYALE?

FURTHER DEBATE

Batman v Wolverine?

Superman v Professor X?

Wonder Woman v Storm?

X-MEN

Three reasons the X-Men would win the battle: They have a more **DIVERSE POWER SET**, they have a brilliant leader, and they have **BETTER FACIAL HAIR**. Justice League really only has two biggies: Superman and Green Lantern. Besides them, you're left with the question-able relationship of Batman and Robin, and the even more questionable relationship of the Wonder Twins, whose transformations into a bucket of water and pelican would not fare well against a pissed-off Wolverine. The rest of the league consists mainly of second-string heroes like Mister Miracle and Blue Beetle. Even Superman and Green Lantern can be vanquished with the aid of kryptonite and the color yellow, respectively. You can bet Professor X has gone shopping for a new kryptonite-bedazzled yellow jumpsuit.

JUSTICE LEAGUE

Other than an occasionally moody Batman, the Justice League members have their personal demons and **SUPERPOWERS UNDER CONTROL**. They also have the **LOVE AND SUPPORT OF THE PEOPLE**. The same cannot be said for the X-Men, who can best be described by one word: *issues*. Rogue's got problems with intimacy (no touching), the soap opera love triangle of Cyclops, Wolverine, and Jean Gray leaves any of them vulnerable to acts of betrayal, and the list goes on. Plus, a good chunk of the X-Men are mere X-boys and X-girls, experiencing puberty's hormonal shifts and all its accompanying volatile and petulant behavior. Professor X will be too busy babysitting to focus on fighting Superman—who will earn MVP in this one.

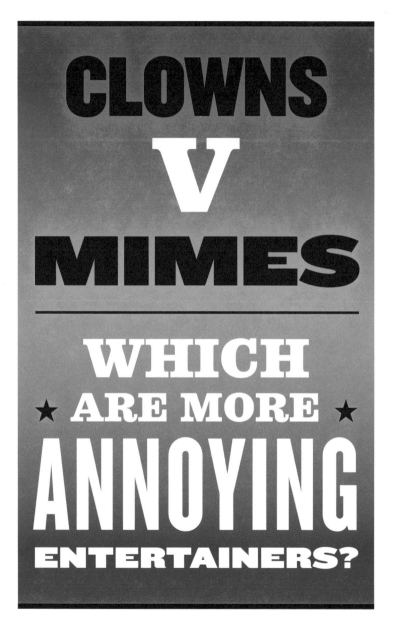

CLOWNS

Clowns are respectable members of society: They offer birthday party entertainment, they provide valuable **RODEO SERVICES**, and they carpool. Mimes? There are few things that are simultaneously scary and annoying, but mimes fit the bill. It's easy to feel bad for mimes because they're always trapped in boxes or struggling to walk through windstorms. But they do it to themselves! A mime is an **IRRITATING NINJA**. They're silent, they wear black, disguise their faces, and while they can't kill you, it feels like torture to watch them. Down with mimes! (Either by simulated stairs or escalator.)

MIMES

DIDN'T YOU KNOW?

FUN FACTS ABOUT MARCEL MARCEAU (WORLD'S MOST FAMOUS MIME)

- He was part of the French Underground and helped children escape from Nazi Germany to Switzerland.

- He was an interpreter under General Charles De Gaulle.

- Michael Jackson modeled the moonwalk after Marceau's walk against the wind.

CAST OF *GREASE*

John Travolta, Olivia Newton-John, Stockard Channing, and the rest of the gang at Rydell High had **MORE TALENT** in their pompadours and Pink Lady jackets than their *High School Musical* counterparts combined. They also had more **EXPERIENCE**, since all of the actors playing high schoolers in the movie were, like, thirty-five at the time. Before Scientology, thinning hair, and a prodigious gut reduced him to donning drag in *Hairspray*, Travolta **BROKE THE MOLD** as far as teen idols go. He offered an oddly comical, self-deprecating riff on the Italian-American stereotype. Plus, he could really act, and he sported some serious moves. Zac Efron is boring and has annoying hair.

CAST OF *HIGH SCHOOL MUSICAL*

The cast of *HSM* has ethnic **DIVERSITY**, and that's an insurmountable advantage in a song-and-dance contest against an all-white cast. Zac Efron is so cool that he doesn't need to spell his name with a "k," and Vanessa Hudgens has already proven that she **HAS THE GOODS** (even without those leaked Internet photos). The supporting cast of *HSM* is equally, if not more, talented. By contrast, the sidekick role of Kenickie in *Grease* was played by Jeff Conaway of *Celebrity Rehab* fame.

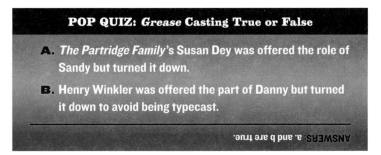

POP QUIZ: *Grease* Casting True or False

A. *The Partridge Family*'s Susan Dey was offered the role of Sandy but turned it down.

B. Henry Winkler was offered the part of Danny but turned it down to avoid being typecast.

ANSWERS: a. and b are true.

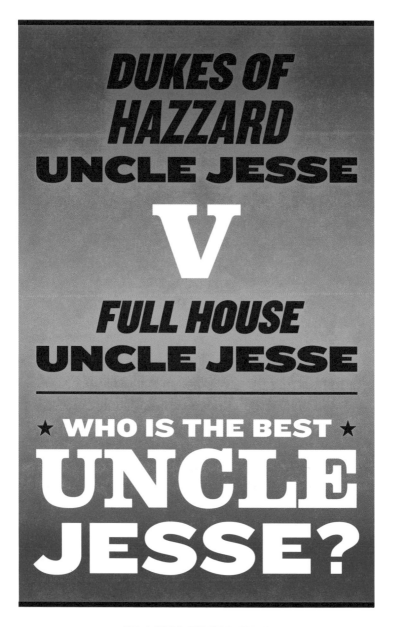

DUKES OF HAZZARD
UNCLE JESSE

V

FULL HOUSE
UNCLE JESSE

★ WHO IS THE BEST ★
UNCLE
JESSE?

DUKES OF HAZZARD
UNCLE JESSE

The *Dukes of Hazzard* Uncle Jesse was a tough-but-wise **VOICE OF REASON** in an otherwise corrupt county. While the Duke patriarch believed in letting boys be good ol' boys, he was **VIGILANT** enough to keep Daisy from getting pregnant and fatally stretching out her Daisy Dukes. And if an Uncle Jesse can be judged best by the hot young women around him (and that's probably the best way to judge an Uncle Jesse), then Jesse Duke gets the nod. No eventual taboo hotness of the Olsen twins can equal the turning-boys-into-men sex appeal of Catherine Bach's **SHORT SHORTS**.

FULL HOUSE
UNCLE JESSE

The *Full House* Uncle Jesse had one of the greatest heads of hair in the history of mankind. As played by John Stamos, the **WELL-COIFFED** Uncle Jesse Katsopolis was both a rock star and an upstanding citizen. After his sister's untimely passing, he proved himself a **DEVOTED AND LOVING** uncle by helping to raise her children. He endured Danny Tanner for their sake, and his sacrifices meant that he reached **MATURITY** at a much younger age than Jesse Duke. I mean, Jesse Duke used to run moonshine with Boss Hog! Alcoholism is a real problem in Hazzard County, and that's just not cool.

DIDN'T YOU KNOW? The Uncle Jesse Test

Want to know if you are too old to date someone? Ask the question, "Who is Uncle Jesse?" If the answer is John Stamos and you were thinking *Dukes of Hazzard*, yep, you're too old.

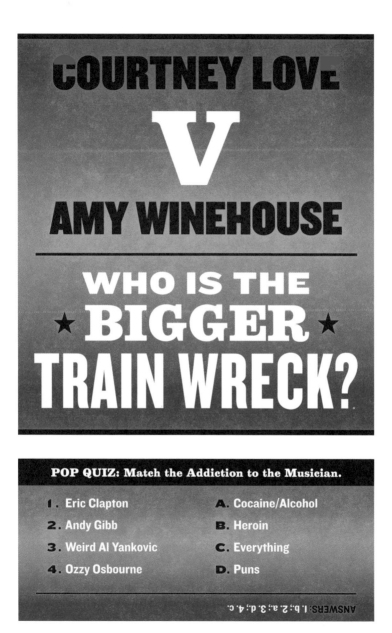

COURTNEY LOVE

V

AMY WINEHOUSE

WHO IS THE
★ BIGGER ★
TRAIN WRECK?

POP QUIZ: Match the Addiction to the Musician.

1. Eric Clapton   A. Cocaine/Alcohol

2. Andy Gibb   B. Heroin

3. Weird Al Yankovic   C. Everything

4. Ozzy Osbourne   D. Puns

ANSWERS: 1. b.; 2. a.; 3. d.; 4. c.

COURTNEY LOVE

Courtney Love is a trailblazer of **CELEBRITY DYSFUNCTION**, truly the Rosa Parks of train wrecks, whose sordid track record (and track marks) makes Amy Winehouse look like Amy Grant. Let's compare: Winehouse admits to having problems with depression and eating disorders; Love admits to taking **HEROIN** while pregnant. Advantage: Love. Winehouse was sentenced to twenty-eight days in rehab; Love was sentenced to six months in state-ordered **LOCKDOWN**. Advantage: Love. Winehouse got into a fistfight with her husband, leaving him bloodied; Love may have been instrumental in the death of a musical genius who was the voice of his generation. Advantage: Love. Hell, Love even earned a Golden Globe nomination for playing a drug addict in *The People vs. Larry Flynt* (to prepare, she spent months learning how to act *less* drugged-out).

AMY WINEHOUSE

Amy Winehouse has more **"CRAZY"** in her beehive than Courtney Love has in her entire body. Despite a relatively brief career, Winehouse has amassed a list of addictions longer than her snaggletooth. And no trip to rehab will stop her from stumbling around in a bra in public or picking at her **BEDSORES** like the druggie diva she is. Love, by contrast, is an accomplished actress. You know what Winehouse does on film? Smokes **CRACK**. And let's not forget that Winehouse is only in her twenties and already probably has the emphysema-riddled lungs of an eighty-year-old coal miner.

KING KONG

V

GODZILLA

WHO WOULD WIN ★ IN A ★ MONSTER BRAWL?

WILDCARD: Who's the Real Winner in This Battle?

Halliburton. That's right, Halliburton. Any way you slice it, the people who are really going to benefit are contractors like Halliburton, who will be rewarded with large contracts to rebuild the cities these two will inevitably destroy. They may even be the ones who set the whole thing up. Wouldn't put it past 'em.

KING KONG

The advantage goes to Kong on **ALERTNESS**. Having just awakened from an underwater slumber, Godzilla is bound to be more than a little groggy. And really, how much monstrous destruction can you accomplish when you're just coming to your senses? Next point: Kong has limbs that are perfectly **SUITED FOR CLIMBING TALL BUILDINGS**, whereas Godzilla's stubby little arms are pretty much useless. Like a cat outmaneuvering a dog, Kong finds sanctuary by climbing. But unlike a cat (at least my cat), Kong has **RIPPLING MUSCLES** and devastating strength with which to pummel both his chest and Godzilla as he pounces down from the top of a skyscraper. Prediction: **A K.O. FROM K.K.**

GODZILLA

The advantage goes to Godzilla on **CRANKINESS**. The fact that Godzilla just awoke from a seemingly eternal slumber should not be held against him. On the contrary, it's only going to make him crankier. And as we all know, a cranky lizard is a **DEADLY LIZARD**. Godzilla's atomic morning breath is **FULL OF FIRE**, and ape hair is flammable. Even if Kong takes to great heights, Godzilla has ocular ray beams, and, sometimes, (the rules aren't exactly clear) he flies. Godzilla's tough hide and healing abilities will defend against the mad fist-pummeling of the ape. Furthermore, Kong, like so many creatures of passion, can fall prey to the call of womanly flesh. Faced with a tough opponent like Godzilla, an unfocused ape is as good as **MARINATED MONKEY BRAINS**.

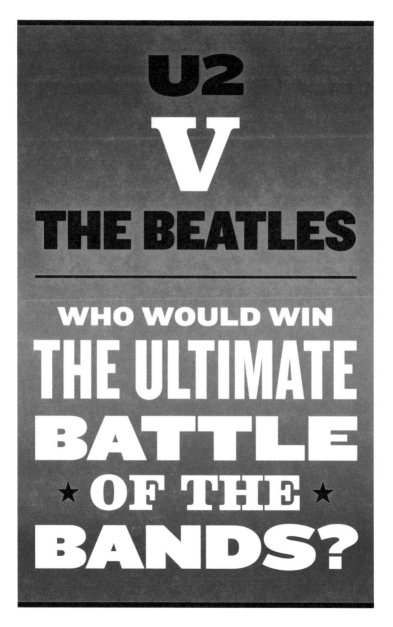

U2

U2 **WINS ON LYRICS** and accompaniment. The band's uniquely brilliant guitar riffs are arguably the soul of the group. And **THE EDGE** goes to, well, himself. The Beatles's inferiority is especially evident in their subpar lyrics, which were always secondary to McCartney ("Yesterday" was originally hatched as "Scrambled eggs, how I like to eat my scrambled eggs"— no joke). Lennon, on the other hand, produced his most poetic work in his later solo efforts. Congratulations, Bono, whatever you're sublimating has made you the **BEST ROCK STAR OF ALL TIME**.

THE BEATLES

The Beatles win on being the **GREATEST BAND EVER**—don't even try to argue otherwise. Their influence on culture and the world as we know it is simply **OFF THE CHARTS**. True, U2 puts on a decent live show, but they're operating with lighting and sound technologies that weren't even around in the Beatles's day. And even without the aid of U2-esque pyrotechnics, the Beatles still had the power to **INCITE MASS HYSTERIA** and fainting. Throw in a fifteen-minute diatribe from Bono in the middle of the concert, and the Beatles are a better live show (adjusted for time).

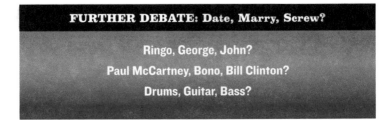

FURTHER DEBATE: Date, Marry, Screw?

Ringo, George, John?
Paul McCartney, Bono, Bill Clinton?
Drums, Guitar, Bass?

DEBATE AMONGST YOURSELVES: BATTLE OF THE BANDS

★ ★ ★ ★ ★ ★ ★ ★ ★ ★ ★ ★

UP 'TIL NOW, THE ARGUMENTS HAVE BEEN MADE FOR YOU. HERE'S YOUR CHANCE TO PUT YOUR DEBATE SKILLS TO WORK. FIND A WORTHY OPPONENT, CHOOSE YOUR SIDE, AND PREPARE FOR BATTLE—FREESTYLE. WHO WOULD WIN THESE MELEES OF THE MUSICALLY MINDED?

Michael Jackson (in his prime) v Prince (in his prime)

Eagles v Wings

The Go-Gos v The Bangles

Diana Ross v Donna Summer

The Grateful Dead v The Doors

Wolfgang Amadeus Mozart v Johann Brahms

Marvin Gaye v Al Green

The Police v Sting (solo)

Dolly Parton v Shania Twain

Jimi Hendrix v Eddie van Halen

The Beach Boys v The Bee Gees

Barbra Streisand v Celine Dion

Bon Scott of AC/DC v Brian Johnson of AC/DC

Guns 'n' Roses of the '80s v Guns 'n' Roses of the '00s

The Judds v The Dixie Chicks

The Who v The Rolling Stones

The Temptations v New Edition

Milli v Vanilli

SMURFS V CARE BEARS

★ WHO WOULD WIN IN A ★ TOON WAR?

WILDCARD: Three Toon Battle Strategies

DIVIDE AND CONQUER: The Care Bears generally need to be together to prepare their Care Bear Stare. The Smurfs would be wise to separate the enemy with ambush attacks.

REINFORCEMENTS/ALLIANCES: The Smurfs have numbers. But do not forget the Care Bear Cousins, who bring several new species and attack methods to the war, including Cozy Heart Penguin, Brave Heart Lion, and Bright Heart Raccoon.

TERRAIN: If the Smurfs create an offensive, they'd be wise to proceed into the Kingdom of Caring via the Forest of Feelings, where they could employ their guerilla tactics.

SMURFS

Each member of the Socialist Republic of Smurfdom (SRS) knows what it means to **SACRIFICE INDIVIDUAL DESIRES** for the welfare of the Great State. In fact, each Smurf represents a singular quality, providing for a well-rounded army: leadership (Papa); brute force (Hefty); engineering prowess (Handy); munitions (Jokey); distracting high jinks (Clumsy); and narcolepsy (Lazy). Moreover, the Smurfs are **MASTER GUERILLA FIGHTERS**, able to keep their entire village hidden from Man, and they're highly skilled in simple machine weaponry, including catapults, battering rams, and Smurfberry launchers. Their defense is well-tested against repeated **GARGAMEL AND AZRAEL ATTACKS**. Most of all, they are ready to fight, as the 99:1 male-to-female ratio has them all sexually riled up. Put simply, the Smurfs will smurf the smurf out of the Care Bears.

CARE BEARS

The Care Bears's primary weapon, the "Care Bear Stare," projects a powerfully **DEBILITATING RAY OF LOVE, CARE, AND GOOD CHEER** that far exceeds any weapon the Smurfs have in their arsenal. Each Care Bear has a unique **"TUMMY SYMBOL,"** an indelible insignia that specifies an individual bear's duty and purpose. The tummy symbols allow for the spontaneous generation of a number of vital combat apparatuses, such as heart-shaped balloons, rainbow bridges, birthday cupcakes, and distress signals. In the event of a war, Tenderheart Bear and Funshine Bear will lead a charge of **LOVING DESTRUCTION**. Smurfs, prepare to stare into the dark abyss of infinite joy. Winner: Da Bears.

DRACULA
V
FRANKENSTEIN'S MONSTER

WHO WOULD WIN IN A BATTLE TO THE (UN)DEATH?

FURTHER DEBATE

A zombie v A mummy?

Bigfoot v Twenty leprechauns?

Vampire with a sprained ankle v Wolfman after just
breaking up with his girlfriend?

DRACULA

Both erudite and smooth-talking, Dracula boasts not only **CENTURIES OF WISDOM**, but also a degree in the black arts (with a minor in drama) from the Academy of Scholomance in the Carpathian Mountains. Dr. Frankenstein's creation, however, suffers from the same weakness that hinders so many monsters: a severe and crippling lack of speed. Like mummies and zombies, the monster's sluggishness makes him vulnerable. His odd gait and difficulty finding properly fitting shoes make him **EASILY ESCAPABLE**, especially when you can **TURN INTO A BAT**. Frankenstein's monster is like a gangly seven-footer in the NBA: He may play good defense and hustle for proverbial loose balls, but there are just natural limits to his agility and speed.

FRANKENSTEIN'S MONSTER

Frankenstein's monster is slow, we'll grant you that. But here's the thing: What happens when a member of the undead bites a creature that has been artificially raised from the dead? Nothing, that's what. This **IMPERVIOUSNESS IS THE SECRET WEAPON** of all slow, lumbering monsters, and it leads to a **SHOCK FACTOR THAT IS AS PARALYZING** as poisonous venom. Watch how it plays out: Sneak-attack bite from Dracula. No reaction. Paralyzing shock then seizes Dracula to the point where he can't even turn into a bat. Frankenstein's monster **CLOBBERS THE VAMP** over the head. Wooden stake through the heart. The impaler becomes the impalee, and, finally, eternal peace for Dracula.

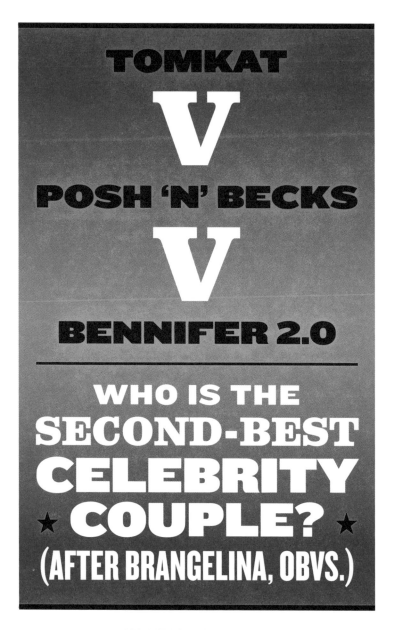

TOMKAT: TOM CRUISE AND KATIE HOLMES

PROS: Hollywood power player, height (Katie), Suri
CONS: Scientologists, couch-jumping tendencies, craziness

POSH 'N' BECKS:
VICTORIA "POSH SPICE" BECKHAM AND DAVID BECKHAM

PROS: Likely athletic ability of progeny, British accents, fashion sense, superhuman good looks
CONS: Lack of depth, overly manicured hair, possible toppling due to extramarital affairs and huge fake boobs on tiny anorexic frame

BENNIFER 2.0:
BEN AFFLECK AND JENNIFER GARNER

PROS: Cheekbones, height, tendency to avoid limelight
CONS: Movie choices, addiction, tendency to avoid limelight

WILDCARD: Fictional Celebrity Supercouples Whose Supercouple (or Portmanteau[1]) Name Would be a Fish

Albacore (Jessica Alba and Corey Feldman)

Katfish (Kat Von D and Laurence Fishburne)

Sardean (Sarah Michelle Gellar and Dean Cain)

Hallebut (Halle Berry and Boutros Boutros-Ghali—
alternative name, Boutros Boutros-Halle)

Moray (Demi Moore and Ray Liotta)

Bonus: Natalie Portman plus Tony Danza = Portmanto.

[1] A portmanteau is a word or name that results from the combination of two words. A common example is "brunch."

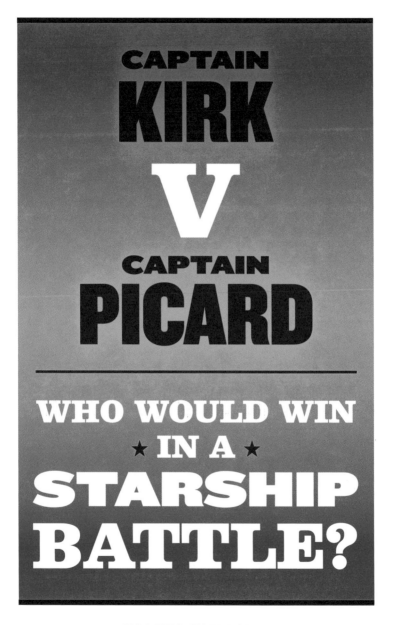

CAPTAIN KIRK

Kirk has all the physical weapons and tricks of a young, virile man: clasped double fist-hammers to opponents' backs, overdramatic diving somersaults, exaggerated karate chops—you know, all the **BEST HAND-TO-HAND FIGHTING** maneuvers the twenty-third century has to offer. Kirk has a dark, dangerous side, **A MUGATO BEAST**–side, if you will (see Episode 45: "A Private Little War"). Not only is he the more interesting person, but his **BRAVADO** is a necessary quality of a *Starship* captain. Picard, on the other hand, is an old man. He is a "stun" to Kirk's "kill."

CAPTAIN PICARD

Don't be fooled by the chrome dome; Picard is quite **VIRILE**. He has **GRAVITAS** and the whole Shakespearean thing, while Kirk's got the weightiness of a Bazooka Joe comic. By the way, can you imagine all the bizarre galactic venereal diseases Kirk must have contracted? Treating those must have taken 80 percent of Dr. McCoy's time. Picard has fended off the Borg juggernaut, saved the Bynar home world, and managed a larger multigalactic staff with conviction and aplomb. Picard would **EFFORTLESSLY TAKE DOWN** the melodramatic Kirk.

FURTHER DEBATE

SPOCK v **DATA**: Who would win in poker?

DR. MCCOY v **WORF**: Who would make the better *American Idol* guest judge?

SCOTTY v **SULU**: Who would you rather do?

DEADHEADS

V

PARROTHEADS

★ WHO ARE THE BETTER ★
FANS?

POP QUIZ:
Which Are Real Names for Fans of Rock Bands?

DOORKNOBS (The Doors)

WHOVILLE (The Who)

MILKERS (Dead Milkmen)

PHISHBAIT (Phish)

GANGBANGERS (Kool and the Gang)

ANSWER: None are real, thank goodness.

DEADHEADS

The Grateful Dead had only one Top 40 hit in three decades ("Touch of Gray"), but they are one of the **TOP-GROSSING LIVE ACTS** in history. For Deadheads, music is about tapping into deep, **SPIRITUAL WELLS** and experiencing other planes of consciousness. For Parrotheads, music is about tapping into kegs and "Cheeseburgers in Paradise." Deadheads immortalized the VW Bus as a symbol of **THE COUNTERCULTURE**, while Parrotheads drove VW Cabriolets and commercialized the cool out of what Deadheads had left their psychedelic teddy bear mark on. Besides, Jimmy Buffett has to hit us over the head with "Why don't we get drunk and screw?" To Deadheads, **FREE LOVE IS ASSUMED**. And they'll do it minus the rum hangover.

PARROTHEADS

Parrotheads are often mocked for their perceived lack of dedication compared to that of Deadheads. And it's true. They don't travel from city to city for every single show like their Deadhead counterparts—because they **HAVE ACTUAL JOBS** that don't entail selling homemade veggie burritos and hemp jewelry! That's right, while Deadheads have a daily routine of waking-and-baking, bongo-playing, and more baking, Parrotheads are contributing **MEMBERS OF SOCIETY** who spur economic growth via their mass Tommy Bahama consumption. And let's be honest, who would you rather hook up with? A braless hippie chick who hasn't showered or shaved since Jerry Garcia died in '94, or a **COCONUT-BRA WEARING** divorcee who gets a nip-and-tuck every spring?

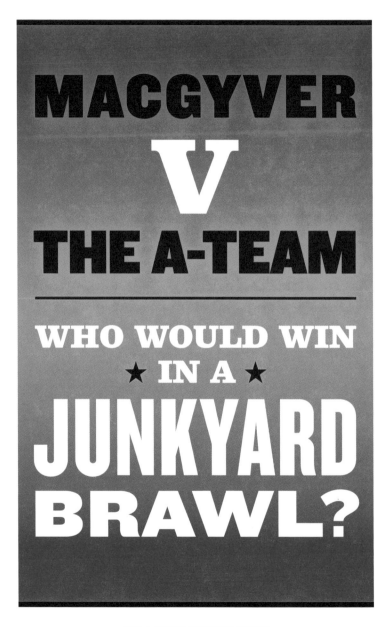

MACGYVER
V
THE A-TEAM

WHO WOULD WIN
★ IN A ★
JUNKYARD
BRAWL?

MACGYVER

MacGyver is so clearly the **APOTHEOSIS OF RESOURCEFULNESS** that his name has become a verb, meaning "to ingeniously create something out of seemingly useless things." And MacGyver is no softy, either. As an agent for the Department of External Services, he's **RESCUED HOSTAGES**, destroyed equipment, and gathered intelligence. Unlike the A-Team, **HIS MORAL CODE IS CLEAR** and unwavering, and his actions are dictated with the confidence and unanimity of one mind. Give a man a fish and he eats for a day. Give MacGyver a fish, and he'll use it to deactivate a bomb.

THE A-TEAM

The A-Team **HAS BALANCE AND SYNERGY**: one-quarter cheeky leadership (Hannibal), one-quarter brute but comical strength (B.A. Baracus), one-quarter smooth **CONFIDENCE** (Faceman), and one-quarter post-traumatic stress disorder (Murdock). Go ahead and try to imprison the A-Team in a barn or county jail. Then sit back and enjoy the welding montage and the ensuing rampage from handcrafted cabbage shooters and flame-throwers. These guys are hardened **VIETNAM VETS**. MacGyver is an unapologetic gun control advocate whose weapon of choice is a Swiss Army knife. Good luck fighting off B.A. with your corkscrew and plastic toothpick.

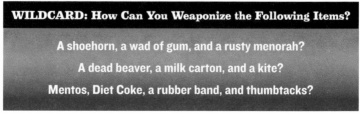

WILDCARD: How Can You Weaponize the Following Items?

A shoehorn, a wad of gum, and a rusty menorah?
A dead beaver, a milk carton, and a kite?
Mentos, Diet Coke, a rubber band, and thumbtacks?

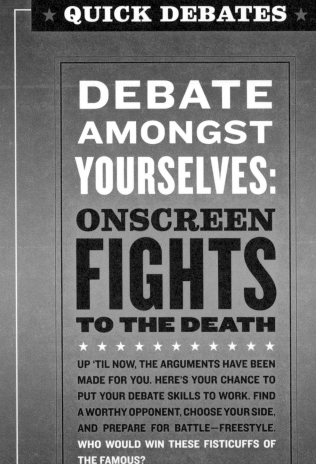

DEBATE AMONGST YOURSELVES: ONSCREEN FIGHTS TO THE DEATH

★ ★ ★ ★ ★ ★ ★ ★ ★ ★ ★

UP 'TIL NOW, THE ARGUMENTS HAVE BEEN MADE FOR YOU. HERE'S YOUR CHANCE TO PUT YOUR DEBATE SKILLS TO WORK. FIND A WORTHY OPPONENT, CHOOSE YOUR SIDE, AND PREPARE FOR BATTLE—FREESTYLE. WHO WOULD WIN THESE FISTICUFFS OF THE FAMOUS?

Spiderman v Batman

The Death Star v The Borg Queen Vessel

Sarah Connor v Ellen Ripley

Alien v Predator (in a game of Texas Hold'em poker)

Lassie v Benji

Ellen DeGeneres v Tyra Banks

Hannibal Lecter v Norman Bates

Chuck Norris v God

Charlie Chaplin v Darth Maul

Neo v Luke Skywalker

Dirty Harry v Indiana Jones

The *Sex and the City* girls v The *Golden Girls*

The Jonas Brothers v The Baldwin brothers

Rocky v Jake La Motta of *Raging Bull*

John McClane of *Die Hard* v Greedo

Jackie Chan v Bruce Lee

Maximus Decimus Meridius (the Gladiator) v Zorro

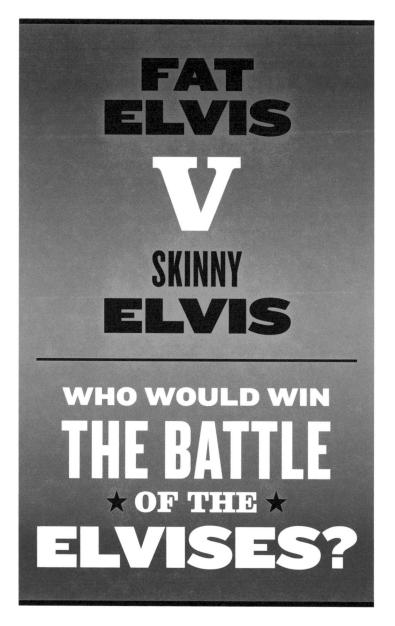

FAT ELVIS V SKINNY ELVIS

WHO WOULD WIN THE BATTLE ★ OF THE ★ ELVISES?

FAT ELVIS

Fat Elvis, when you think about it, is the true icon. The crazy **SIDEBURNS**, the sequined leisure suits, the shades: Elvis became **LARGER THAN LIFE** when he became larger than average. His songs were still great ("Suspicious Minds," "Burning Love") and his maturity shone through in socially minded songs like "In the Ghetto." Plus, we all know that imitation is the highest form of flattery, and most Elvis impersonators choose fat Elvis over his svelte predecessor. Skinny Elvis soured his rep with bad movie after bad movie, while fat Elvis **TORE UP VEGAS** like a casino buffet.

SKINNY ELVIS

Skinny Elvis = young, pretty Elvis = pompadour Elvis = the real Elvis. Fat Elvis ceased his **TRADEMARK GYRATIONS** for fear of throwing out his hip and died on the can from a pill overdose. He was the *Phantom Menace* of rock 'n' roll, the unraveling and perversion of a **LEGACY** that by any right should have been impossible to ruin. The reason there are more impersonators of fat Elvis is because it's a hell of a lot easier to imitate a fat, untalented person than a supple, talented one.

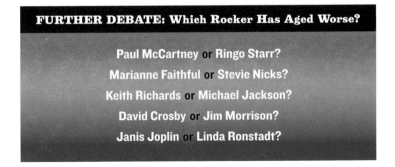

FURTHER DEBATE: Which Rocker Has Aged Worse?

Paul McCartney **or** Ringo Starr?

Marianne Faithful **or** Stevie Nicks?

Keith Richards **or** Michael Jackson?

David Crosby **or** Jim Morrison?

Janis Joplin **or** Linda Ronstadt?

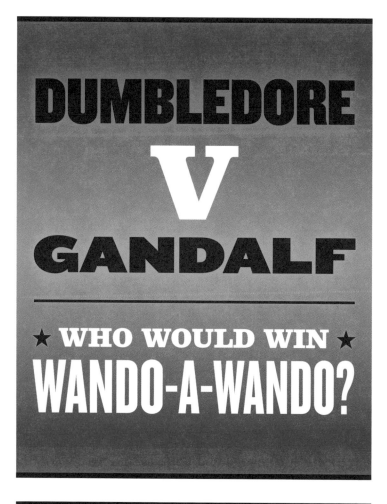

DUMBLEDORE

V

GANDALF

★ WHO WOULD WIN ★
WANDO-A-WANDO?

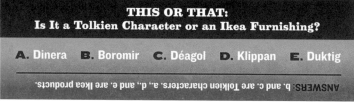

THIS OR THAT:
Is It a Tolkien Character or an Ikea Furnishing?

A. Dinera   **B.** Boromir   **C.** Déagol   **D.** Klippan   **E.** Duktig

ANSWERS: b. and c. are Tolkien characters. a., d., and e. are Ikea products.

DUMBLEDORE

Some corporate wizards will tell you, "Those who can't do magic, teach magic, and those who can't teach magic, teach Potions." But nothing could be further from the truth. Dumbledore has the edge on Gandalf because **THROUGH TEACHING, HE HAS GAINED MASTERY**. The true extent of his power lies hidden, revealed only in times of great need. Like his pet phoenix, Dumbledore has risen from **IMPOSSIBLE DEPTHS**. No ivory tower academic, this super-wizard has been pivotal in the defeat of He-Who-Must-Not-Be-Named on more than one occasion and always with great poise, for his knowledge of spells and magic is second to none. Gandalf barely made it out alive battling a Balrog, for Morwen's sake!

GANDALF

In a battle of magic, Gandalf is the heavy favorite. To put it in simple terms, Gandalf (*see also* Olórin; Tharkûn; Mithrandir) was one of the **DIVINE** and **POWERFUL** Maiar of Valinor—an **IMMORTAL** Istari (a.k.a. wizard) fated to serve the Valar and the creator Ilúvatar, and to prevent the evil Sauron from controlling Middle-Earth. He might look feeble and crotchety, but the old-man act conceals his extraordinary physical and magical strength—dude fought evil for more than two thousand years! Having been trained by Nienna (a.k.a. the patron of mercy) in the gardens of Irmo, Gandalf knows when to whip out the magic and when to chill. Even the ruler of Lothlórien, the Lady of Lórien (*see also* the Lady of the Galadhrim; Galadriel), deemed Gandalf the **WISEST** of the wizards. Obviously, Gandalf wins.

GUITARISTS

V

DRUMMERS

★ WHO WOULD WIN ★

THE BATTLE *IN*

THE BAND?

DIDN'T YOU KNOW? Fun with Mnemonics

A STANDARD TUNED GUITAR HAS THE STRINGS ORDERED E, A, D, G, B, E.
HERE'S A FEW HELPFUL WAYS TO REMEMBER IT:

Ed Asner Destroyed Greg Brady's Ears

Existential Angst Deadens Gary Busey's Excellence

Electric Aardvarks Don't Generate Bountiful Energy

GUITARISTS

Kids grow up wanting to be **ERIC CLAPTON**, **JIMI HENDRIX**, and John Lennon. No one grows up wanting to be Max Weinberg or Ringo Starr. That's like dreaming of becoming a backup quarterback. And, honestly, how difficult can the drums really be if they can be played by a guy with one arm (Def Leppard's Rick Allen)? While we're asking questions, **WHAT'S GOING ON WITH DRUMMER GLOVES?** How much hand protection do you need to grip a couple of sticks that are about the weight and girth of two pretzel logs? Drum solos are admittedly a demanding test of physical and psychological endurance . . . for the concertgoer who is forced to patiently sit through them. (Rim shot, please.)

DRUMMERS

You know what the heart of rock 'n' roll does? That's right, it *beats*. It doesn't *strum*. The drummer is both physically and musically the **BACKBONE OF THE BAND** (think Don Henley for the Eagles, Keith Moon for The Who, Phil Collins for Genesis, and **ANIMAL FOR DR. TEETH AND THE ELECTRIC MAYHEM**). Let's try a little experiment: If you take a band and lose the guitarist, you have Keane (a hugely successful group with three number-one albums). But if you take a band and lose the drummer, you have, well, Simon and Garfunkel (a glee club without the glee). Of course, drummers are capable of playing nonstop for hours because they are in amazing physical shape.

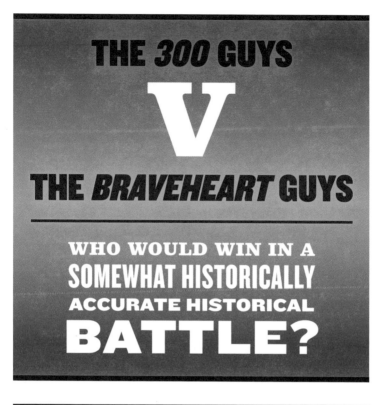

THE *300* GUYS

V

THE *BRAVEHEART* GUYS

WHO WOULD WIN IN A
SOMEWHAT HISTORICALLY
ACCURATE HISTORICAL
BATTLE?

FURTHER DEBATE: Would You Rather . . .

Live in sepia tone like the world of *300* or have to wear *Braveheart*-style make-up everyday?

Listen to an inspiring battle speech given by a drunk Mel Gibson or a 4-year-old?

Go on a date with someone who speaks with an obviously fake Scottish accent or someone who dresses like a character from *300*?

THE *300* GUYS

Maybe a bit of creative license was used in claiming that three hundred Spartans withstood an army of a million Persian soldiers, but historians have confirmed the lopsided nature of the battle of Thermopylae, as well as King Leonidas's **TACTICAL GENIUS** and sheer will. Just as they did with the Persians, the Spartans would funnel Team Braveheart into the narrow terrain (tempting them with Scotch, perhaps?) and then **TAKE THEM DOWN** with their expert archers. William Wallace may have balls, but the Spartan king took down barbarians, giant rhinos, and war elephants— not to mention making a God-King bleed.

THE *BRAVEHEART* GUYS

Okay, so the Spartans are ripped, but everyone looks **MORE RIPPED** when they're sepia-toned. Either way, if you're noticing their bods at all, it means they are not wearing a lot of armor. They are dressed for "summer battle," leaving them vulnerable. The *Braveheart* guys are not only properly dressed for battle, but William Wallace would give them the peppiest of pep talks and inspire them to come from behind and **WIN WITH THE GUERILLA TACTICS** they used against the English armies. As Wallace said: *Sons of Scotland, they can take your lives, but they can't take your American Express.* No wait. . . . *You can pick your nose, and you can pick your friends, but you can't pick your friend's freedom!* . . . Or something like that.

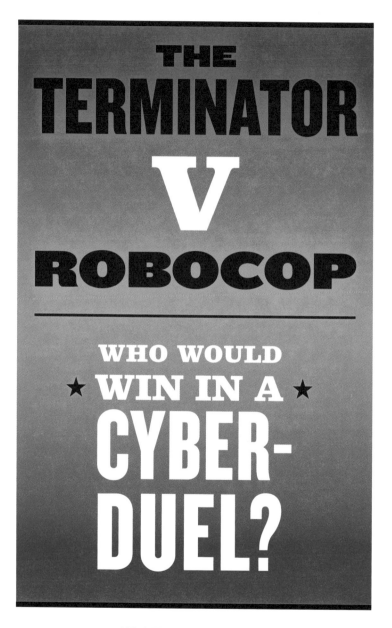

THE
TERMINATOR
V
ROBOCOP

WHO WOULD
★ WIN IN A ★
CYBER-
DUEL?

THE TERMINATOR

To be clear, we're talking about the T-800 from the original *Terminator* (the robot designed to have absurdly **BULGING MUSCLES** and a monotone **AUSTRIAN ACCENT**, not the gelatinous mercury-like blob of sequel fame). Metallic head to metallic head, the Terminator **HAS THE EDGE IN ALL CATEGORIES**: He's faster, stronger, and has better catchphrases. Plus, Robocop is part human and falls prey to distracting human emotions. Weapons-wise, the Terminator's arsenal of machine guns and grenade launchers have the edge on Robocop's Auto-9, and it's just a matter of what clever line will be delivered upon victory— maybe: "Time to recycle."

ROBOCOP

Don't let the muscles fool you. The Terminator is the cyborg equivalent of a dumb jock. Robocop's A.I. lets him respond in complete sentences, and he's **PART HUMAN**, allowing him to **ADAPT TO NEW SITUATIONS**. Robocop is an iPhone to the Terminator's Commodore 64. His arsenal includes missile launchers and machine guns, and he's even been known to strap on a jetpack. With armor made of titanium layered with Kevlar, Robocop can withstand bombs, heat, and round after round of bullets. Terminator terminated.

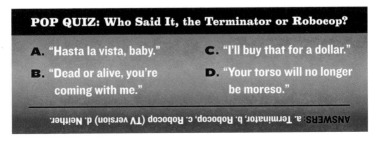

POP QUIZ: Who Said It, the Terminator or Robocop?

A. "Hasta la vista, baby."

B. "Dead or alive, you're coming with me."

C. "I'll buy that for a dollar."

D. "Your torso will no longer be moreso."

ANSWERS: a. Terminator, **b.** Robocop, **c.** Robocop (TV version) **d.** Neither.

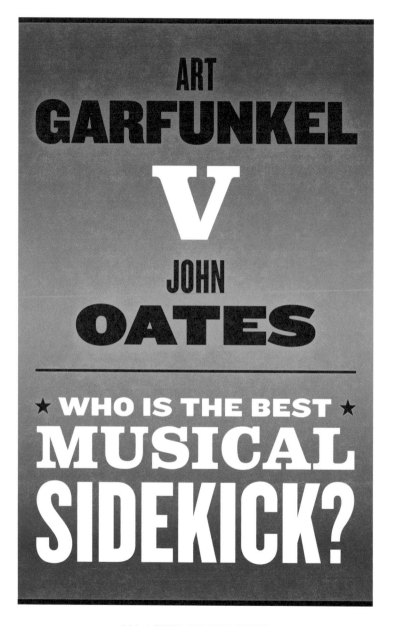

ART GARFUNKEL

You can't spell Garfunkel without the **"FUNK."** Garfunkel was a man destined for success because he saw success (a.k.a. Paul Simon) and paired up with him. Simon and Garfunkel's biggest hit is **"BRIDGE OVER TROUBLED WATER,"** which spent six weeks at number one and won the Grammy award for "Song of the Year." Garfunkel sings it SOLO. His **ETHEREAL TENOR VOICE** was featured on the soundtrack to the generation-defining film *The Graduate*, whereas Hall & Oates's "Rich Girl" was featured on an episode of the TV series *Hunter*. There's really nothing to debate: Garfunkel worked with Paul Simon. He knew Paul Simon. And you, Daryl Hall, are no Paul Simon.

JOHN OATES

You better watch out, Artie boy, cause 'Stache Oates—he'll chew you up! The **"MANEATER"** had ten number-one hits, sported a **MUSTACHE IMITATED BY MILLIONS**, and was the glue that held "We Are the World" together. Where was Garfunkel on that album? Did he decide to sit out that famine? Let's face it, without Simon, Garfunkel would just be that guy with the frizzy bouffant who takes karaoke night WAY too seriously. And he doesn't even play an instrument. Come to think of it, he never takes his hands out of his pockets.

DIDN'T YOU KNOW?

Paul Simon was inducted into the Rock and Roll Hall of Fame twice: as a duo with Garfunkel (1990) and as a solo artist (2001).

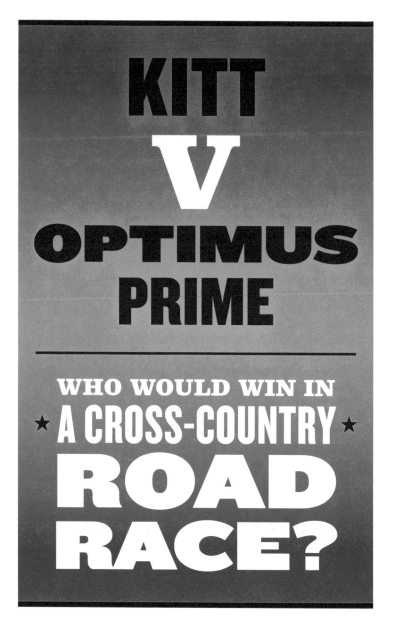

KITT
V
OPTIMUS
PRIME

WHO WOULD WIN IN
★ **A CROSS-COUNTRY** ★
ROAD
RACE?

KITT

Two words: *turbo boost*. On the open road, KITT can reach **SPEEDS OF 300 MPH**. And let's not forget how **FULLY LOADED** KITT is: grappling hook and winch, electromagnetic hyper-vacuum brakes, pyroclastic lamination, and self-controlled door locks that can be activated in shady neighborhoods. KITT can even drive on water! Besides, Optimus has terrible gas mileage, which, in this day and age, translates into a seriously expensive trip. KITT is the autonomous auto of choice, and as long as a drunk David Hasselhoff doesn't try to take the wheel, it's KITT who will take the checkered flag.

OPTIMUS PRIME

It might be obvious here, but with Prime, there's more than meets the eye. Prime's **TRANSFORMING ABILITY** allows him to tackle rugged terrain in robot form, leaping, climbing, and bounding over mountains, whereas KITT has to stick to the roads. In addition to being indestructible, **THE LEADER OF THE AUTOBOTS** is known for being routinely punctual. And don't be misled by KITT's snobby faux-English accent. As far as artificial intelligence goes, Optimus has the edge. After all, he is the leader of a race. And he'll be the leader of this race, too. Roll out.

WILDCARD: Worst-Selling Transformers

A-LINE: Transforms into a retainer.

GEORGE: Transforms into a George Foreman Grill.

PEDRICON: Transforms into one of those things that measures your shoe size.

CHAPTER ★ FIVE ★

SCIENCE

&

NATURE

METRIC SYSTEM

V

THE AMERICAN
SYSTEM OF MEASUREMENT

★ HOW DO THEY ★
MEASURE UP?

POP QUIZ:
Which Are Real Historic Units of Measurement?

A. CUBIT: A distance of about 45 centimeters

B. MICKEY: The smallest detectable movement of a computer mouse, approximately equal to 0.1 mm

C. PLELN: The distance from your neck to the front yard

D. FATHOM: A distance of about six feet, originally based on the length between a man's outstretched arms

ANSWERS: a, b, and d. are real units of measurement.

METRIC SYSTEM

Before the metric system, every region had a different way of measuring things, resulting in immeasurable confusion. So in **1790**, the French National Assembly commissioned the Academy of Science to create a **SIMPLE**, **DECIMAL-BASED** system that would alleviate the need for Trapper Keepers with conversion charts on the inside flaps. Naturally, every nation adopted the metric system—except, that is, the United States, who stuck with their own system (probably because "one foot" seemed like a pretty good length for a large sandwich at Subway). And what a **LOGICAL SYSTEM** it is. After all, if twelve inches makes a foot, it makes perfect sense that three of those make a yard and 5,280 of those make a mile and . . .

AMERICAN SYSTEM

Irrational American **UNILATERALISM** and **INDEPENDENCE** is what makes us American. So when every other country adopts the metric system, damn straight we'll do our own thing. How can we measure the depth of our independence if we are using a measurement system given to us by the French? No, merci, we'll wash down our freedom fries with a **12-OUNCE BUDWEISER**. These metric missionaries have been trying to force their system down our throat, centimeter by centimeter, for decades, and you can bet your Euros we're **NOT GOING TO BUDGE AN INCH** (except for our drug dealers with their defiant and un-American kilos and liters). What's next, spelling theater "theatre"?

JUPITER

V

SATURN

WHICH PLANET IS THE ★ COOLEST? ★

JUPITER

Jupiter is King of the Planets. When it comes to size, number of moons (upward of sixty-three), **BIG, RED SPOTTINESS**, and any other measure of planetary greatness, J-dogg's number one. At 88,846 miles (142,984 km) in diameter, it's **ELEVEN TIMES THE SIZE OF EARTH**. Saturn, by contrast, always comes in second. The Miss Congeniality of planets also suffers from a spare tire around its midsection (technically called an *oblate spheroid*) caused by its rapid orbit. Congratulations, Saturn, on being the solar system's only fat planet (and sorry, but those rings aren't hiding anything).

SATURN

Saturn's got a set of rings that would make Liberace blush. We're talking **MAJOR GALACTIC BLING**: ice, electrostatic bolts, and tholin purities. Rappers would die for that (and have). And Jupiter has nothing on Saturn when it comes to **WIND SPEEDS**, which can reach 1,100 miles per hour (1,800 km per hour), significantly faster than those on Jupiter (400 miles per hour, or 643 km per hour). Plus, Saturn is the only planet in the solar system with **A WARM POLAR VORTEX**. Take that and shove it up your big, red spot!

FURTHER DEBATE

Mercury v Uranus?

Mars v Neptune?

Pluto: True planet or dwarf planet?

ONE POLAR BEAR

Polar bears have no natural predators, and, thus, **NO FEAR**. They're the Great White Hope of bears and the **LARGEST LAND PREDATOR** on the planet—male bears can grow to ten feet tall and 1,400 pounds. They are **EXPERT SWIMMERS**, so if a battle goes naval, they can go bobbing for koalas. Koala bears, by contrast, aren't even bears; they're marsupials. As in kangaroos. Here's a fatal fact: The tiny-brained koalas spend sixteen hours a day sleeping. Easy targets, they'll soon be sleeping eight more hours a day. By the end of this battle, the polar bear's white fur will be red, and the koalas will be cast eternally "down under."

FIFTY KOALA BEARS

Numbers, baby, numbers. Koalas, bear or no bear, have claws, too. Twenty of them. Multiply that by fifty koalas, and you get a total of one thousand painful swipes to the jugular. Plus, they've got **RAZOR-SHARP TEETH** for clipping leaves. Sure, they move slowly, and, yes, they're cuddly, but koalas have a mean streak that leads to **AGGRESSIVE BARKING** and fighting, especially during mating season. Koalas also have **OPPOSABLE THUMBS**— perfect for eye-gouging. So maybe thirty to forty of the little cuddlepusses take one for the team. But in the end, ten victorious koalas will be forgoing eucalyptus for something meatier.

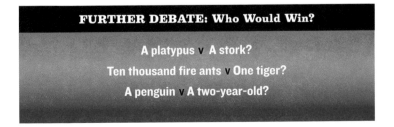

FURTHER DEBATE: Who Would Win?

A platypus **v** A stork?
Ten thousand fire ants **v** One tiger?
A penguin **v** A two-year-old?

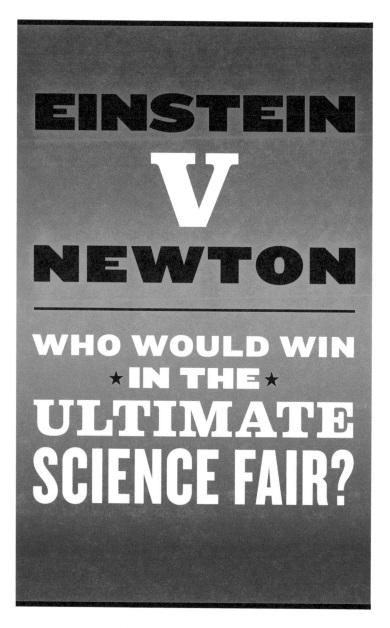

EINSTEIN
V
NEWTON

WHO WOULD WIN
★ IN THE ★
ULTIMATE
SCIENCE FAIR?

EINSTEIN

$$R_{pw} - \frac{1}{2} g_{pw} R + g_{pw}A = \frac{8\pi G}{c^4} T_{pw} = Einstein\ rulz$$

NEWTON

$$\vec{F} = \frac{d\vec{p}}{dt} = \frac{d}{dt}(m\vec{v}) = \vec{v}\frac{dm}{dt} + m\frac{d\vec{v}}{dt} = Einstein\ sucks\ it!\ Q.E.D.$$

POP QUIZ: True or False

Both Einstein and Newton believed in God.

ANSWER: False

NEWTON was devoutly religious and produced more work on Biblical hermeneutics than the natural science he is remembered for today.

EINSTEIN on God: "My position concerning God is that of an agnostic. I am convinced that a vivid consciousness of the primary importance of moral principles does not need the idea of a law-giver, especially a law-giver who works on the basis of reward and punishment."

CROCODILE

Crocs have the strongest bite in the animal kingdom— **FIVE THOUSAND POUNDS** per square inch. They also have **BRAINS**, possessing a developed cerebral cortex that allows them to learn and strategize. According to the Discovery Channel's *Animal Face-Off*, a lion would likely be unable to deliver a fatal bite to the crocodile because of the croc's thick, **ARMOR-LIKE SKIN**. In fact, various cultures have used crocodile skin as armor in battle. The croc, using that cortex we mentioned, will wait in the water and surprise the lion, clamping on the neck, and delivering a **DEATH ROLL**. By the way, don't bother trying to run in zigzags to get away. That's a myth.

LION

The lion is the **KING OF THE JUNGLE**, which is a feat since it lives in the savannah. That's quite a rep, like Springsteen being popular in Europe. The lion is not dumb. It knows to stay on land in this battle. Crocs do not chase after prey; whereas lions have been known to **HUNT AND KILL** giraffes, hippos, and even rhinoceros. But here's where it gets interesting. A lion's fatal blow comes most often by **FORMS OF ASPHYXIATION**: a strangling bite or—and this would be the case on the croc—by covering the nostrils and mouth in its jaws. And, as evidenced by the rubber bands used to keep a captive croc's mouth closed, it doesn't take much pressure to restrain him. Yeah, a rubber band. What a croc.

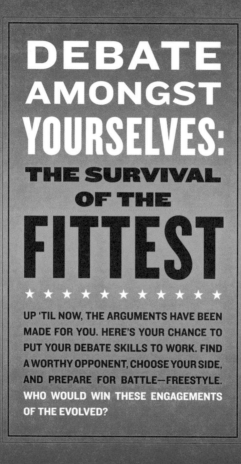

DEBATE AMONGST YOURSELVES:
THE SURVIVAL OF THE
FITTEST

★ ★ ★ ★ ★ ★ ★ ★ ★ ★ ★ ★

UP 'TIL NOW, THE ARGUMENTS HAVE BEEN MADE FOR YOU. HERE'S YOUR CHANCE TO PUT YOUR DEBATE SKILLS TO WORK. FIND A WORTHY OPPONENT, CHOOSE YOUR SIDE, AND PREPARE FOR BATTLE—FREESTYLE. WHO WOULD WIN THESE ENGAGEMENTS OF THE EVOLVED?

A giant squid v A great white shark

Global warming theory v Trickle-down economics theory

A gorilla v A bull

One buffalo v Five rottweilers

Invention of the atomic bomb v Invention of the television

Bald eagle v Bengal tiger

Watson and Crick v Alexander Fleming
(discovered the Double Helix)   (discovered penicillin)

A cow v A chihuahua

Volcanoes v Earthquakes

Five hundred fireflies v One tortoise

A kitten v A baby panda

A Venus flytrap v A poison hemlock

LEFT

V

RIGHT

★ **WHICH IS THE BETTER** ★

DIRECTION?

WILDCARD: Are You Left- or Right-Brained?

LEFT BRAIN FUNCTIONS	RIGHT BRAIN FUNCTIONS
Logic	Insight
Words and language	Imagination
Scientific skills	Spatial perception
Reasoning	Symbols and images
Number skills	Feelings

LEFT

Left-handed people represent a disproportionately large number of **HIGH ACHIEVERS**. Just ask Bill Clinton, Oprah Winfrey, Michelangelo, Angelina Jolie, and Ned Flanders, all of whom are lefties. In fact, in 2006, researchers at Lafayette College and Johns Hopkins University found that left-handed men are 15 percent richer overall than right-handed men. And this is just the logical argument (**LOGIC IS FOUND** in the left side of the brain, by the way). On a gut level, left is just cooler. It's the Mac to the right's PC. Lefty is a quirky nickname. Righty? Sounds ridiculous. The left side **IS WHERE THE HEART IS**, literally and metaphorically. What organ is on your right? The appendix? Go left, young man.

RIGHT

Right is so clearly the superior direction that the word itself has come to mean **"CORRECT"** or "morally appropriate" in languages around the world. The Latin word for right-handed is *dexter*, as in "dexterity." In Irish, *deas* means "right side" and "nice." Contrast that with "left," which in English connotes communism. The Latin word for "left" is *sinestra*, from which we derive our word "sinister." In Ireland, left-handers are called *ciotóg*, which comes from the Gaelic for "clumsy-ass stupid." All this is not coincidence. We distrust left because in our intuitive time-space understanding, left is our communal weak side. Left is the past, while **RIGHT IS THE FUTURE**. And left turns are a pain in the ass.

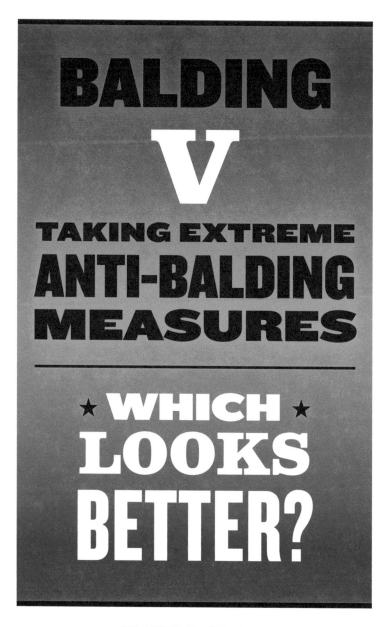

BALDING

V

TAKING EXTREME

ANTI-BALDING
MEASURES

★ WHICH ★
LOOKS
BETTER?

BALDING

A wonderful thing happened for bare-headed men in the 1980s: Michael Jordan went bald. With a few fateful swipes of a razor, he legitimized the shaved head as a **BONA FIDE STYLE** choice for men. Twenty-plus years later, depilation is still in style, man. It **GIVES YOU EDGE**. Look at some of the great bald guys out there: Stone Cold Steve Austin, Tiki Barber, the security guy on Springer, Kojak, Curly Neal—the list is endless.

TAKING EXTREME ANTI-BALDING MEASURES

Everyone bemoans the cheesy horror of the "comb-over," but other than the most egregious of its kind (*see also* The Donald), the comb-over is actually effective in presenting the illusion of both hair and power (*see also* Rudy Giuliani; Vladimir Putin). And make fun of hair plugs all you want, but the bottom line is that Joe Biden is vice president *because they work*! Baldness might suffice for the ultimate accepters (*see also* Gandhi; Confucius), but hair is like fudge; some is better than none. Plus, with modern medical miracles like Propecia and Rogaine, it is worth fortifying the hairline front and pushing back the Bald Blitzkrieg. When you're bald, it's your identity; you're the bald guy, the George Costanza. And anything else you might achieve will be secondary to that moniker.

WILDCARD: Not-So-Effective Ways to Hide a Bald Spot

Eyebrow Comb-Over

The Back Hair Comb-Over

The "Oh My Gosh!" Hands-on-Your-Head-in-Amazement-All-the-Time Comb-Over

SUMMER
V
WINTER

★ WHICH ★
IS THE
BETTER
SEASON?

SUMMER

Summer is like a **FOUR-MONTH-LONG FRIDAY** where everybody is half-assing it at work. It's synonymous with **SUN**, **SURF**, and **SKIN**. It's the time for taking vacations, barbecuing, and playing lawn darts. Winter, by contrast, is the time for Seasonal Affective Disorder (SAD) and deep depressions. Not to mention holiday weight gain, long dark nights, snowballs in the face, and hypothermia.

WINTER

Of course there's skiing, **SLEDDING**, and the wonder of the holiday season. But you know what's best about winter? It's when you go inside after being outside in the cold and feel like **YOU'VE ACCOMPLISHED SOMETHING**. You're like, "Man, we made it." And you treat yourself to a cup of **HOT CHOCOLATE** and another plate of cookies. You deserve it! When the weather is warm and the days are long, laziness and overeating just don't have the same indulgent quality. And don't get me started on sunburns. Not to mention getting sand in your bathing suit.

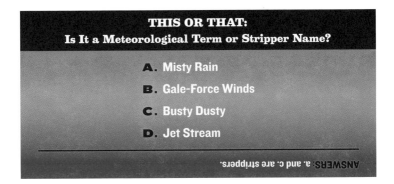

THIS OR THAT:
Is It a Meteorological Term or Stripper Name?

A. Misty Rain

B. Gale-Force Winds

C. Busty Dusty

D. Jet Stream

ANSWERS: a. and c. are strippers.

BRUNCH

V

WIND

★ WHO WOULD WIN IN ★

A SHOWDOWN

BETWEEN TWO

COMPLETELY

UNRELATED THINGS?*

(*NOTE: This matchup is the result of a logistical snafu.)

BRUNCH

With brunch, you have the best of **BREAKFAST** foods and **LUNCH** foods. You can treat yourself to a **WHOLE CULINARY JOURNEY**, starting with eggs and bacon, moving onto a bagel with smoked salmon, proceeding to steak, and finishing up with fresh fruit or perhaps a cookie. Best of all, brunches allow you to **DRINK MIMOSAS OR BLOODY MARYS**, one of the few instances in which day-drinking is not only socially permissible but encouraged. Wind isn't even edible, and you certainly can't linger over it while nursing a hangover and sporting bedhead on a **SUNDAY MORNING**.

WIND

Wind is the **ENERGY SOURCE** of the future. It offers an **ECO-FRIENDLY** alternative to fossil fuels. There's nothing like a light breeze on a mild summer day to relax your mind and restore your spirit. And wind is essential for **FLYING KITES**. You can't fly kites with brunch, can you? As any dietician will tell you, brunch is bad. If you want to lose weight, you're supposed to eat several light meals throughout the day rather than gorging on one giant meal. So, I'll take my breakfast and lunch separate, thank you very much. Then I'll sit my skinny butt in a field and enjoy a **REFRESHING BREEZE**.

FURTHER DEBATE

George Washington Carver v Tom Hanks?

Marbles v Kangaroos?

Subtraction v The smell of grass?

INDEX

50 Cent, 101

'80s v '90s, 94–95

300 (movie), 140–141

300 guys v *Braveheart* guys, 140–141

1972 Miami Dolphins v 1985 Chicago Bears, 34–35

1975 Cincinnati Reds

1985 Chicago Bears, 34–35

1998 New York Yankees

A

A-Team, The, 95, 130–131

Abdul-Jabbar, Kareem, 61

AC/DC, 119

Actors turned musicians v musicians turned actors, 100–101

Adams, Douglas, 59

Aerosmith, 102

Affleck, Ben, 125

Agassi, Andre, 52–53

Alba, Jessica, 125

Alexander the Great, 89

Algerian (font), 27

Ali, Muhammad, 40–41

Alien, 133

Allen, Rick, 139

American system of measurement, 150–151

Andersen, Hans Christian, 31

Animal Face-Off (TV show), 159

Apples v oranges, 54–55

Arial (font), 27

Art Garfunkel v John Oates, 144–145

Atkins, Dr., 49

Attila the Hun, 89

Austin, Steve, 165

B

Bach, Catherine, 111

Balding v taking extreme anti-balding measures, 164–165

Baldwin brothers, 133

Bangles, The, 119

Banks, Tyra, 133

Barber, Tiki, 165

Bates, Norman, 133

Batman, 104–105, 133

Baylor, Elgin, 61

Beach Boys, The, 119

Beatles, The, 116–117

Beckham, David, 125

Beckham, Victoria "Posh Spice," 125

Bee Gees, The, 119

Beer v wine, 36–37

Belushi, Jim, 101

Belushi, John, 101

Benji, 133

Bennifer 2.0, 124–125

Berry, Halle, 125

Biden, Joe, 165

Bird, Larry, 52, 60, 61

Björn Borg v Andre Agassi, 52–53

Black, 22–23

"Blaze of Glory" (song), 103

Blue Beetle, 105

Bol, Manute, 35

Bon Jovi, Jon, 102–103

Bonaparte, Napoleon, 89

Bond, James, 98–99

Bono, 117

Books, movie versions of, 18–19

Books v movie versions of books, 18–19

Booty Call (movie), 52

Borg, Björn, 52–53

Borg Queen Vessel, 133

"Born to Run" (song), 103

Boston Celtics v LA Lakers, 60–61

Botticelli, Sandro, 12

Bourne, Jason, 98–99

Boutros Ghali, Boutros, 125

Bradley, General Omar Nelson, 89

Brahms, Johann, 119

Braveheart (movie), 140–141

Braveheart guys, 140–141

"Bridge Over Troubled Water" (song), 145

Bronzino, Il, 12

Brosnan, Pierce, 99

Bruce Springsteen v Jon Bon Jovi, 102–103

Brunch v wind, 168–169

Bryant, Kobe, 61, 63

Buchanan, Pat, 79

Buffett, Jimmy, 129

Buonarroti, Michelangelo, 13, 163

Burger King v McDonaldland characters, 70–71

"Burning Love" (song), 135

Bush, George W., 84–85

C

Cain, Dean, 125

Campbell's Soup Cans (Warhol), 31

Canada v Switzerland, 86–87

Captain Kirk v Captain Picard, 126–127

Captain Picard, 126–127

Care Bears, 120–121

Carey, Mariah, 101

Carlin, George, 31

Carroll, Lewis, 31

Carter, Jimmy, 84–85

Carver, George Washington, 169

Cast of *Grease* v cast of *High School Musical*, 108–109

"Centerfield" (song), 102

Chan, Jackie, 133

Channing, Stockard, 109

Chaplin, Charlie, 133

Cheers (TV show), 95

Che Guevara, 89

Child, Julia, 49

Clapton, Eric, 112, 139

Cleese, John, 99

Clinton, Bill, 84, 117, 163

Clowns v mimes, 106–107

Coffee, 66–67

Collins, Phil, 139

Conaway, Jeff, 109

Confucius, 165

Connery, Sean, 99

Connor, Sarah, 133

Cookie Monster v Pac-Man, 38–39

Cooper, Michael, 61

Cosell, Howard, 63

Costanza, George, 165

Courtney Love v Amy Winehouse, 112–113

Cousy, Bob, 61

Cowens, Dave, 61

Craig, Daniel, 99

Craig, Jennie, 49

Crocodile v lion, 158–159

Crosby, David, 135

Crosswords v sudoku, 68–69

Cruise, Tom, 125

Csonka, Larry, 35

Cyclops, 105

Cyrus, Miley, 19

D

Da Vinci, Leonardo, 13

Dalton, Timothy, 99

Danza, Tony, 125

David (Michelangelo), 13

Day-Lewis, Daniel, 99

De Gaulle, Charles, 107

Dead Milkmen, 128

Deadheads v Parrotheads, 128–129

Death Star, 133

DeGeneres, Ellen, 133

Dey, Susan, 109

Die Hard (movie), 133

Dion, Celine, 119

Ditka, Mike, 35

Dixie Chicks, The, 119

Donnie Darko (movie), 51

Doors, The, 119, 128

Dr. Seuss v Shakespeare, 16–17

Dracula v Frankenstein's monster, 122–123

Drummers, 138–139

Duke, Daisy, 111

Duke, Uncle Jesse, 111

Dukes of Hazzard (TV show), 110–111

Dukes of Hazzard Uncle Jesse v *Full House* Uncle Jesse, 110–111

Dumbledore v Gandalf, 136–137

E

Eagles (band), 119, 139

Easter Bunny v Santa Claus, 50–51

Efron, Zac, 109

Eisenhower, Dwight, 89

Einstein, Albert, 156–157

Einstein v Newton, 156–157

Elizabeth I, Queen of England, 89

Emma (Austen), 31

Ernest Hemingway v Norman Mailer, 24–25

Exclamation point, 14–15

F

Faithful, Marianne, 135
Fat Elvis v skinny Elvis, 134–135
Feldman, Corey, 125
Fishburne, Laurence, 125
Flanders, Ned, 163
Fleming, Alexander, 161
Fogerty, John, 102
Fonts, 26–27
For Whom the Bell Tolls (Hemingway), 25
Fountain (Duchamp), 31
Frankenstein's monster, 122–123
Full House (TV show), 110–111

G

Gandalf, 136–137
Gandhi, Mohandas, 76–77, 165
Gandhi v Mother Teresa, 76–77
Garamond (font), 27
Garcia, Jerry, 129
Garner, Jennifer, 125
Garfunkel, Art, 139, 144–145
Garnett, Kevin, 61
Gates, Bill, 13
Gaye, Marvin, 119
Gellar, Sarah Michelle, 125
Genesis (band), 139
Genghis Khan, 89
George Washington v Abraham Lincoln, 92–93
Gibb, Andy, 112

Gilmore Girls (TV show), 25
Giuliani, Rudolph, 165
"Glory Days" (song), 103
Go-Gos, The, 119
God, 133
The Godfather (movie), 52
Godzilla, 114–115
Golden Girls (TV show), 133
Goodrich, Gail, 61
Goudy Stout (font), 27
Gozolli, Benozzo, 12
The Graduate (movie), 145
Graf, Steffi, 53
Grant, Amy, 113
Grant, General Ulysses S., 89
Grant, Hugh, 99
The Grapes of Wrath (Steinbeck), 31
Grateful Dead, The, 119, 129
Gray, Jean, 105
Grease (movie), 108–109
The Great Gatsby (Fitzgerald), 31
Greedo, 133
Green, Al, 119
Green Lantern, 105
Gretzky, Wayne, 63
Guitarists v drummers, 138–139
Guns 'n' Roses, 119

H

Hairspray (movie), 109
Hall, Daryl, 145
Halliburton, 114

Hamburger, 64–65
Hamill, Dorothy, 52
Hammurabi v U.S. Founding Fathers, 82–83
Hanks, Tom, 169
Harding, Tonya, 52
Harrison, George, 117
Hasselhoff, David, 147
Havlicek, John, 61
Heinsohn, Tom, 61
Hemingway, Ernest, 24–25
Hendrix, Jimi, 119
Henley, Don, 139
High School Musical (movie), 108–109
Hilton, Paris, 71
Hitchhiker's Guide to the Galaxy (Adams), 59
Hogan, Hulk, 56–57
Holmes, Katie, 125
Hopkins, Anthony, 99
Hot dog v hamburger, 64–65
Howe, Gordie, 63
Hudgens, Vanessa, 109
Hulk Hogan v The Rock, 56–57
Hunter (TV series), 145

I

Idol, Billy, 102
Iron Sheik, 57

J

Jackson, Michael, 13, 107, 119, 135
James Bond v Jason Bourne, 98–99
Jane Eyre (Brontë), 31
"Janie's Got a Gun" (song), 102

Jimmy Carter v George W. Bush, 84–85
Joan of Arc, 89
Johnson, Brian, 119
Johnson, Dennis, 60, 61
Johnson, Don, 101
Johnson, Magic, 61
Jolie, Angelina, 163
Jonas Brothers, 133
Jones, Sam, 61
Joplin, Janis, 135
Jordan, Michael, 52, 165
Judds, The, 119
Julius Caesar, 89
Julius II, Pope, 13
Jupiter v Saturn, 152–153
Justice League, 104–105

K

Katsopolis, Uncle Jesse, 111
Keane, 139
Kennedy, John F., 92–93
King Kong v Godzilla, 114–115
KITT v Optimus Prime, 146–147
Koala bears, 154–155
Kool and the Gang, 128

L

LA Lakers, 60–61
La Motta, Jake, 133
Lassie, 133
Lecter, Hannibal, 133
Lee, Bruce, 133
Lee, General Robert E., 89

Left v right, 162–163
Lennon, John, 117, 139
Leonard, Sugar Ray, 63
Leonidas of Sparta, 89
Lewinsky, Monica, 79
Lincoln, Abraham, 92–93
Lion, 158–159
Liotta, Ray, 125
Lord of the Rings (movie), 52
Love, Courtney, 112–113
Lovett, Lyle, 101

M

MacArthur, General Douglas, 89
Maccabeus, Judas, 89
MacGyver v The A-Team, 130–131
Madame Bovary (Flaubert), 19
Madden, John, 63
Madison, James, 83
Mailer, Norman, 24–25
Manet, Édouard, 31
Marceau, Marcel, 107
Mary I, Queen of Scotland, 89
Maul, Darth, 133
McBeal, Ally, 103
McCartney, Paul, 117, 135
McClane, John, 133
McDonald, Ronald, 71
McDonaldland characters, 70–71
McHale, Kevin, 60, 61
McMahon, Jim "The Punky Q.B.", 35
Meat eaters v vegetarians, 58–59

Meridius, Maximus Decimus, 133
Metric system v American system of measurement, 150–151
Michelangelo v Leonardo, 12–13
Mikan, George, 61
Milli Vanilli, 119
Mimes, 106–107
Mister Miracle, 105
Mona Lisa (da Vinci), 13
Monet, Claude, 31
Moon, Keith, 139
Moore, Demi, 125
Moore, Roger, 99
Morrison, Jim, 135
Moses, 13
Mother Teresa, 76–77
Mozart, Wolfgang Amadeus, 119
Muhammad Ali v Mike Tyson, 40–41
Murphy, Eddie, 41, 101
Murray, Bill, 71
Musicians turned actors, 100–101

N

Nader, Ralph, 78–79
The Naked and the Dead (Mailer), 25
Navratilova, Martina, 63
Neo, 133
New Edition, 119
Newton, Isaac, 156–157
Newton-John, Olivia, 109
Nicholson, Jack, 25

Nicklaus, Jack, 63
Nicks, Stevie, 135
Ninja, 90–91
Norris, Chuck, 133

O

Oates, John, 144–145
Olsen twins, 111
One polar bear v fifty
    koala bears, 154–155
O'Neal, Shaquille, 61
Optimus Prime,
    146–147
Oranges, 54–55
Osbourne, Ozzy, 112

P

Pablo Picasso v Vincent
    Van Gogh, 20–21
Pac-Man, 38–39
Paper, 72–73
Parcells, Bill, 89
Parish, Robert, 60–61
Parks, Rosa, 113
Parrotheads, 128–129
Parton, Dolly, 119
The Partridge Family
    (TV series), 109
Patton, General
    George S., 89
Payton, Walter
    "Sweetness," 35
The People vs. Larry
    Flint (movie), 113
Pepper, 46–47
Perot, Ross, 78–79
Perry, William "The
    Refrigerator," 35
Petraeus, General
    David, 89
Phelps, Michael, 63
Phish, 128
Picasso, Pablo, 20–21

Pieta (Michelangelo),
    13
Polamalu, Troy, 52
Polar bear, 154–155
Police, The (band), 119
Portman, Natalie, 125
Posh 'n' Becks, 124–
    125
Powell, General Colin,
    89
Predator, 133
Presley, Elvis, 134–135
Prince, 119
Professor X, 104–105
Pryor, Richard, 31
Putin, Vladimir, 165

Q

Quayle, Dan, 84
Question mark v
    exclamation point,
    14–15

R

Raging Bull (movie),
    133
Rare (steak), 42–43
Ray, Rachael, 71
Red v black, 22–23
Renaissance man,
    12–13
"Rich Girl" (song),
    145
Richards, Keith, 135
Right, 162–163
Ripley, Ellen, 133
Robin, 105
Robinson, Sugar Ray,
    63
Robocop, 142–143
Robocop (movie),
    142–143
Rock, The, 56–57

Rock v paper v scissors,
    72–73
Rocky, 133
Rogue, 105
Rolling Stones, The,
    119
Rommel, Erwin, 89
Ronstadt, Linda, 135
"Rosanna" (song), 27
Ross, Diana, 119
Ross Perot v Ralph
    Nader, 78–79
Rubik's Cube, 95
Russell, Bill, 61

S

Salt v pepper, 46–47
Samurai v ninja, 90–91
Sanders, Colonel, 71
Santa Claus, 50–51
Sartre, Jean-Paul,
    80–81
Saturn, 152–153
Scissors, 72–73
Scott, Bon, 119
Scott, Byron, 61
Sedaris, David, 31
Seinfeld (TV show), 95
Seppuku, 91
Sesame Street (TV
    show), 39
Sex and the City (TV
    show), 133
Shakespeare, William,
    17
Shields, Brooke, 53
Shula, Don, 35
Simon, Paul, 139, 145
Singletary, Mike
    "Samurai Mike," 35
Sistine Chapel, 13
Skinny Elvis, 134–135
Skywalker, Luke, 133

Sistine Chapel, 13

Skinny Elvis, 134–135

Skywalker, Luke, 133

Slater, Christian, 25

Slippery When Wet (album), 103

Smurfs (TV show), 95

Smurfs v Care Bears, 120–121

Socrates, 80–81

Spitz, Mark, 63

Springsteen, Bruce, 102–103

Stamos, John, 111

Starr, Ringo, 135, 139

Stewart, Martha, 49

Sting, 101, 119

Street Fighter (video game), 95

Streisand, Barbra, 101, 119

Sudoku, 68–69

Summer, Donna, 85, 119

Summer v winter, 166–167

Summer Games v Winter Games, 44–45

Superman, 104–105, 133

Sun Tzu, 89

"Suspicious Minds" (song), 135

Switzerland, 86–87

T

Taking extreme anti-balding measures, 164–165

Tanner, Danny, 111

Tea v coffee, 66–67

Teletubbies (TV show), 95

Temptations, The, 119

Terminator (movie), 142–143

Terminator v Robocop, 142–143

Thriller (album), 13

Times New Roman (font), 26–27

TomKat v Posh 'n' Becks v Bennifer 2.0, 124–125

Travolta, John, 109

"Turning Japanese" (song), 102

Twain, Shania, 119

Tyson, Mike, 40–41

U

U2 v The Beatles, 116–117

U.S. Founding Fathers, 82–83

V

Van Gogh, Vincent, 20–21

Van Halen, Eddie, 119

Vapors, The, 102

Vegetarians, 58–59

Verdana v Times New Roman, 26–27

The Village Voice, 25

Von D, Kat, 125

W

Wallace, William, 141

Washington, George, 89, 92–93

"We Are the World" (song), 145

Weinberg, Max, 103, 139

Well-done v rare, 42–43

West, Jerry, 61

White, Jo, 61

"White Wedding" (song), 102

Who, The, 119, 128, 139

Wilde, Oscar, 31

Williams, Serena, 63

Willis, Bruce, 101

Wind, 168–169

Wine, 36–37

Winehouse, Amy, 112–113

Winfrey, Oprah, 163

Wings, 119

Winkler, Henry, 109

Winter, 166–167

Winter Games, 44–45

Wolverine, 104–105

Wonder Twins, 105

Wonder Woman, 104

Wooden, John, 63

Woods, Tiger, 63

Worthy, James, 61

X

X-Men v Justice League, 104–105

Y

Yankovic, Weird Al, 27, 112

Yo Momma v Yo-Yo Ma, 28–29

Yo-Yo Ma, 28–29

Z

Zorro, 133

ACKNOWLEDGMENTS

Thanks to Lindsay Herman for her amazing patience and talent and for doing all the work I should have been doing. Thanks to Quirk, especially Sharyn Rosart, Lynne Yeamans, and Erin Canning. Thanks also to Greg Chaput and Chris Barsanti for pulling the weeds from my words. Much thanks to Eric Immerman and Paul Katz for their contributions. Thanks most, as always, to my mom and to my wife Marisa for everything, and for being so saintly during rough times. You both win.

ABOUT THE AUTHOR

Justin Heimberg writes books, television shows, movies, magazine articles, songs, games, and musicals of his friends' lives. He is the Creative Director and cofounder of Seven Footer Entertainment (sevenfooter.com), a media company specializing in humor, games, and innovative products for kids. He is currently writing for the Fox Network's *The Cleveland Show*. Justin lives with his wife, Marisa, and his two cats, Randall Jones and Harriet Tuftman.